The Pilgrim's Way to St. Patrick's Purgatory

Sculptural Figure with Staff and Bell. White Island.

The Pilgrim's Way to St. Patrick's Purgatory

BY

Eileen Gardiner

ITALICA PRESS
NEW YORK
2010

ITALICA PRESS, INC.
595 Main Street
New York, New York 10044
inquiries@italicapress.com

Library of Congress Cataloging-in-Publication Data
Gardiner, Eileen.
The pilgrim's way to St. Patrick's Purgatory / by Eileen Gardiner.
    p. cm.
Includes bibliographical references and index.
 Summary: "Based on an actual medieval pilgrimage route, this work
traces a contemporary route from Dublin to Lough Derg, Donegal. It
provides a cultural itinerary through Ireland's medieval past with its
surviving, but fragmentary, riches, as it crosses the Irish borders and
landscape, its rivers and lakes"--Provided by publisher.
 ISBN 978-1-59910-187-3 (hardcover : alk. paper) -- ISBN 978-1-59910-167-5
(pbk. : alk. paper) -- ISBN 978-1-59910-164-4 (e-book)
 1. Saint Patrick's Purgatory (Ireland) 2. Christian pilgrims and
pilgrimages—Ireland. 3. Ireland—Religious life and customs. 4. St.
Patrick's Purgatory (Legend) I. Title.
 BX2321.D4G37 2010
 263'.04241693--dc22

                                                           2010003533

FOR A COMPLETE LIST OF ITALICA PRESS TITLES

VISIT OUR WEB SITE AT:

WWW.ITALICAPRESS.COM

CONTENTS

WEB RESOURCES

HOME

http://www.pilgrimswaytopurgatory.org/Site/

STATUS / NEWS

http://stpatrickspurgatory.blogspot.com/

PHOTO GALLERIES

http://www.italicapress.com/index412.html

INTERACTIVE MAP

http://www.italicapress.com/index414.html

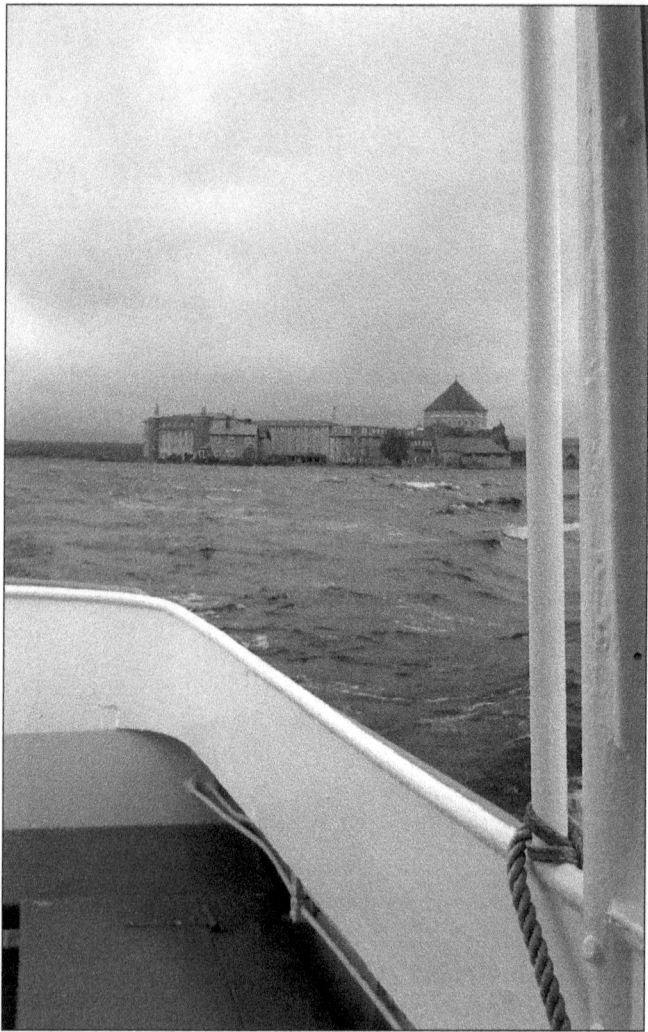

Lough Derg and Station Island.

ILLUSTRATIONS

(Unless otherwise noted, all photos and illustrations are from the Italica Press Archives.)

MAPS

PREFACE

The Pilgrim's Way to St. Patrick's Purgatory traces a route for the modern pilgrim across Ireland and across the boundaries of the Irish Republic and Northern Ireland. It begins in Dublin and ends at Lough Derg in County Donegal, bringing travelers on a journey through the medieval past and the fragmentary riches that remain today. It provides a cultural itinerary that can be traveled by car or bike, on foot, and even partly by boat, through one of the loveliest landscapes of Ireland and Europe.

This publication presents an introduction to the topic, an exploration of a taxonomy of medieval pilgrimage and an overview of what the early pilgrims have told us about the route. It features descriptions of the monuments, relics and saints along the way, as well as a stage-by-stage description of the journey itself. Ancillary materials include travelers' information, an interactive map, a bibliography, a chronology and online photo galleries.

A website (www.pilgrimswaytopurgatory.org), which is a companion to this volume, includes a project status page that presents up-to-date postings on the route and the conversation and scholarship surrounding it. It also includes color illustrations and an interactive map.

My prior — and continuing — work on visions of heaven and hell provided an early acquaintance with St. Patrick's Purgatory through the *Tractatus de*

Purgatorio Sancti Patricii of H. of Saltrey. Combined with this was Italica Press's interest in pilgrimage literature. As some of its first works in the late 1980s, Italica published *The Marvels of Rome, A Guide to the Holy Land* and *The Antiquities of Constantinople*. In 1993, working with William Melczer, it published *The Pilgrim's Guide to Santiago de Compostela*.

Later that same fall in Rome, I was seated at a dinner next to Sir John Leslie. It was not long before I learned that he was the son of Shane Leslie and in fact the owner of Lough Derg. He told me about the landscape around Pettigo, and although it was — at the time — the farthest thing from my mind, he suggested that I should really make the trip to visit the area. I soon found myself pondering how the medieval pilgrimage to St. Patrick's Purgatory would fit into the bigger pilgrimage picture of medieval — and modern — Europe.

It has taken many years to finally get down to the work, but during that time many others have filled in important pieces, so that we can now see that this route through Ireland is an extension of the medieval pilgrimage routes across Europe. It is the newest one identified, and very different from the others, in that its destination is a place of solitude and peace, rather than a thriving town or city. But its appeal is undeniable, and I hope that it will not be long before many more pilgrims are making their way along this route as we first did in May 2009.

ACKNOWLEDGMENTS

With the help of many experts in Ireland, the St. Patrick Purgatory Project has been developed to assemble medieval and early modern evidence in order to establish a clear historical picture and a modern identity for the route and to act as a focal point for further research and discussion.

I am indebted to several libraries and their staffs for help with this project, including the Research Division of the New York Public Library, the Fordham University Libraries, Trinity College Library (Dublin) and the Armagh Public Library.

For assistance with the research that underlies this project, I would like to thank in alphabetical order: William Battersby of Kells; Cormac Bourke, formerly of the National Museum, Belfast; Richard Chambers of White Island; John B. Cunningham of Erne Heritage Tour Guides; Martina Donohue of the Fermanagh Tourist Information Centre, Enniskillen; Michael Doyle of the Office of Public Works; Desi Egan of Pettigo; Doreen Fitzsimmons of the Kells Heritage Centre; Michael Haren, formerly of the Irish Manuscripts Commission; Sir John Leslie; Yvonne Mulligan of the Office of Public Works; Hilary Shaw of the Brederth Sen Jago; and Arthur Spears of Donegal.

I would also like to thank for their help Caroline Bruzelius of Duke University, who introduced me to John Leslie; Stephen Dost of Red Marble Media; John Fleet and Philip Hoskings of CERES; Mark F. Lawless of New York; F. Donald Logan, emeritus of Emmanuel

College, Boston; Deborah Maxwell of Lough Derg;
Pat McDonnell of Dromore; Thurza Mulder of
the Armagh Public Library and her husband Paul
Eliasberg; Robert O'Neill of Boston College; David
Richtmyer of Boston College; Hilary Shaw and the
members of the Bredereth Sen Jago of Cornwall;
Paudie Wall of Slane; and Margaret Wilson of the
National Museum, Edinburgh. I would also like to
thank Crona Connolly of the Original Print Gallery,
Dublin, for a wonderful conversation that provided
an important insight into the pilgrimage experience.

I would particularly like to thank Prior Richard
Mohan and Maureen Boyle of Lough Derg for the
opportunity to first visit Station Island and for the
subsequent correspondence that provided additional
information and materials.

And finally, my thanks to Ron Musto for sharing
this adventure and all the other adventures, and
also for being a constant source of great photos,
excellent advice and careful analysis, and for the best
companionship.

CHAPTER 1.
INTRODUCTION

St. Patrick's Purgatory is a cave on Station Island in Lough Derg, County Donegal, Ireland. It is a very old and well known pilgrimage site, despite its remoteness. The pilgrims' journey to St. Patrick's Purgatory is mentioned clearly in texts from as early as 1185 and shown on maps from all over Europe as early as the fifteenth century. It has long been famous as a penitential site, where pilgrims endured hardship to atone for their sins.

The earliest records for St. Patrick's Purgatory predate the time when the Christian otherworld or afterlife included purgatory. Before the twelfth century, the otherworld comprised only heaven and hell. The purgatory on Station Island was not an otherworldly purgatory, but, like most pilgrimage sites, it was an actual place where repentant Christians repaired to try to avoid hell in the otherworld.

Stories about this purgatorial cave are allegedly even more ancient than the surviving documents, and they are colored by the legends of saints and heroes. Over time these legends and descriptions of visions of, and journeys to, heaven and hell, which reportedly took place at Lough Derg, were conflated with the actual *purgatorium* to both create and reinforce a popular notion that St. Patrick's

Purgatory was an entrance to the otherworld — the world of heaven, hell and eventually an otherworld purgatory.

❖

From at least the twelfth century, pilgrims came from all across Europe to visit the purgatory, and they still come every summer to this lonely lake in Donegal — Lough Derg, or Red Lake.

Today's pilgrim usually comes by car or bus, but in the Middle Ages most pilgrims came by foot, the same way pilgrims traveled to Rome, Jerusalem, Canterbury and Santiago de Compostela. Records of their journeys tell us of the route they took to reach this destination in the northwest extreme of this extreme northwest island.

Over time the route varied, and sometimes pilgrims came by boat up the rivers and lakes, or especially later, on horseback. But in the earliest period of pilgrimage to St. Patrick's Purgatory a clear way along old roads passed numerous monasteries offering hospitality to pilgrims.

During the sixteenth century, the monastic heritage of Ireland — with its churches, sculpture and reliquaries — was almost completely destroyed, leaving melancholy ruins throughout the landscape — or leaving no trace at all. The route continued, but there would have been enormous differences from that point because of the political climate, the disappearance of important landmarks, the change in religious practices brought about by the Reformation and Counter-Reformation and, later, by changes in transportation.

Texts, documents, maps and archeological remains form the basis of our evidence for the medieval route. The texts particularly are not without problems: many are not first-hand accounts; they were often recorded by someone other than the pilgrim and often some time after the pilgrimage. Often documents were written to advance a particular agenda, which today may be obscure, rather than to document accurately an incident. Texts often do not agree with each other, and many texts are now lost. However, with these limitations in mind, it is still possible to reconstruct a route across Ireland to Lough Derg that passes through a landscape with enough remains to constitute a pilgrimage way rich in cultural, religious and natural attractions.

All of these materials — texts, maps and fragments of the cultural past — were fruitful in reconstructing the route, but it was also necessary to test it against other well recognized routes to determine whether it shared basic characteristics with those long-distance pilgrimage itineraries. This comparison is presented in the following chapter, "A Taxonomy of Medieval Pilgrimage."

St. Brigid's Well, Lough Derg, with prayer rags on cross.

CHAPTER 2.
A TAXONOMY OF
MEDIEVAL PILGRIMAGE

Christian pilgrimage developed in late antiquity as the faithful traveled far and wide to visit the relics of Christ, His Apostles, the Blessed Virgin and the martyrs.

Evidence for the long duration of pilgrimage in the Christian Church is clear from texts as early as Paula and Eustochium's fourth-century letter from Jerusalem; and from church architecture. From as early as the fourth century three basilicas in Rome had incorporated ambulatories to accommodate the large numbers of pilgrims who circulated through them, performing rituals, taking part in rites and visiting relics. These ambulatories allowed them to pass behind the main altar, without disturbing the liturgy. (McClendon, 23.)

The practice of pilgrimage soon spread from the burial sites of the primary figures in Christianity, to those martyred during the early persecutions to confessors, who confessed to being Christian, but were not martyred. The cult of saints, who were nominated locally during this early period, sprang up across Europe. The remains or relics of saints spread as well, across Spain and France, Italy, Asia Minor and the Holy Land. Relics moved from place to place, sometimes apparently of their own accord, like the body of St. James, or were surreptitiously or even at time forcibly removed in a theft labeled *"furta sacra"* (Geary, 1978). Cathedrals and churches acquired relics in an attempt to accumulate their great spiritual benefits, and also to attract pilgrims. At the same time monasteries offered pilgrims hospitality as they traveled from place to place visiting the remains of holy Christians, expecting that this pious activity would bring them closer to God and salvation.

❖

The best known are the pilgrimages to the Holy Land, Rome and Santiago de Compostela, but we can quickly add such destinations as Mount Sinai, Canterbury, Vezelay, Rouen, Downpatrick, Walsingham, Monte Gargano, Constantinople or Saint-Maximin-la-Sainte-Baume. Furthermore, when plotting the various pilgrimage routes on a map of Europe and the Near East, it becomes clear that these routes interlocked with and extended one another across an entire cultural region beyond any natural, linguistic or even contingent political borders.

From this long tradition of medieval pilgrimage it is possible to establish a taxonomy of pilgrimage, to evaluate the Pilgrim's Way to St. Patrick's Purgatory against this objective standard and to establish its place in this framework.

My comparative research has established fourteen elements to define the essence of medieval Christian pilgrimage sites and routes in this taxonomy.

1. CULT SITE: Pilgrimage is directed toward destinations that are considered special because they are connected with a holy person who can serve as an intercessor for the faithful between the realms of the sacred and the profane. Cult sites were often burial places, where the physical remains of a holy person were laid to rest. The Shine of the Holy Sepulchre of Jesus in Jerusalem achieved cult-site status early, as did the tombs of the Apostles. Burial in the Roman world was always outside the city walls, and the tombs of St. Peter at the Vatican and St. Paul on Via Ostiense were at that time outside the walls of Rome, where we also find the catacombs, the burial sites for the early Christian martyrs and the faithful, who choose to be buried near these Apostles. Churches grew up around and above these burial sites, and both the cemeteries with encompassing churches jointly became places of pilgrimage.

As relics became more portable objects, and as the nature of relics evolved, cult sites were no longer tied to burial places, but moved into cathedrals and churches away from the cemeteries. Eventually relics became almost ubiquitous, and sites of particular significance — usually places associated with miracles or visions — could have relics brought to them and so become designated cult sites.

Lough Derg was initially the site of a monastic community of anchoritic men on Saints Island, under the leadership of St. Dabheoc, who was probably buried there with his followers. Saints Island and St. Dabheoc were eventually eclipsed by Station Island

and the miraculous legend surrounding St. Patrick and his purgatory.

2. CULT FIGURE: All pilgrimage sites had at least one principal cult figure, a saint or holy person (*sanctus/sancta*). Initially cult sites grew up primarily around Jesus and His Apostles, His mother, the early Christian martyrs, and other followers of Christ, like Mary Magdalene. They came to be joined by holy men and women who professed the Christian faith and were deemed by their local communities to have a special connection to God and could therefore intercede with God on behalf of the living (Brown, 1–12).

Even after canonization became a matter of papal approval in the thirteenth century, locally-sanctioned saints continued to draw pilgrims, although those sanctioned by Rome began to have an increasingly important and international profile.

At St. Patrick's Purgatory, Patrick is now the principle cult figure, but this high-profile saint probably displaced the earlier — and local — Donegal saint here, St. Dabheoc.

3. SECONDARY CULT FIGURES: Since the early Christians sought to be buried near the remains of the holy men and women who came before them in places like Rome and Jerusalem, sites often clustered together. Over time, sites were linked, at first by small local routes, like the one that linked Rome's twelve major and minor basilicas, then by longer routes that joined these saints together across greater distances.

In Rome, for instance, among others, Saints Paul, Lawrence, John the Baptist and John the Evangelist, Bartholomew, Stephen and Mary were all represented by major basilicas. In addition, from the early fourth century the Basilica of Santa Croce in Gerusalemme was founded to enshrine the relics of Christ's birth and passion, thus including Christ among the cult figures in Rome, all clustered around the burial place of the first bishop of Rome, St. Peter.

Over 25 saints are associated with the pilgrimage route connecting various regions of France to Santiago de Compostela. These range, for example, from St. Hilary at Poitiers and St. Martin at Tours, to St. Honoratus at Arles, St. Saturninus at Toulouse, St. Leonard at Noblat, and finally to St. James at Compostela.

For St. Patrick's Purgatory, the following secondary saints are associated with the Station Island in particular: St. Brendan, St. Brigid, St. Catherine of Alexandria, St. Columcille and St. Molaise. All of them — but Catherine — are early Irish saints from the sixth through eighth centuries. Catherine, with her international reputation, seems to have displaced St.Adamnan, a local Donegal saint. They are all recognized by penitential "beds," which appear to be the remains of early beehive cells or huts.

As with local saints' shrines along the route to Compostela, along this route we find locations associated with St. Columcille and St. Molaise, but also with St. Cassán, St. Ciarán, St. Erc, St. Feidhlimidh, St. Mac Cuilinn, St. Maedhóg, St. Malachy, St. Nennid and St. Ronan.

4. PRINCIPAL ROUTE: From early guides it is clear that pilgrimage routes crossed Europe and the Near East. In the tenth century Sigeric the Serious recorded his itinerary to Rome. It started at Canterbury, where he was archbishop, and crossed France and Switzerland to Italy. At Aosta it was joined by other routes heading south to Rome. These pilgrimage routes now may have special names, such as Sigeric's Via Francigena, but would have followed long-established trade routes. The same phenomenon is, of course, substantiated for the pilgrim's route to Compostela.

Such a route can be identified in Ireland. It stretched from Dublin north to Drogheda, and there turned west and north up the Boyne and Blackwater Valleys into the Lough Erne region, where it used the lake system and island monasteries to proceed north and west.

5. ALTERNATE ROUTES: In the network of trade routes, many possibilities existed for getting from one place to another, and often more than one pilgrimage route to any site was documented in the Middle Ages. The routes that capture the modern imagination seem often to be those that preserve the most interesting remains through the most agreeable landscapes, but in the Middle Ages travel was difficult and largely on foot, and starting point, season and political climate would have effected a pilgrim's choice. The alternate routes across the Pyrenees provide a good example.

There were also alternate ways to reach Lough Derg: from Donegal in the west, from Armagh in the east through Clogher and from the south, probably from Limerick, along the River Shannon into the Lough Erne basin. (None of these alternate routes, however, appear to conform to the taxonomy outlined here.)

6. STATIONS: As the routes expanded from a walk around Rome or Jerusalem, visiting the important churches and shrines, to long-distance routes across hundreds of miles, identifiable stations would spring up approximately every 20 k or 12 mi — one day's journey apart by foot. Often these would have their own saints and relics, like Conques, where the remains of the martyr Sainte Foy were preserved.

Despite the dissolution of the Irish monasteries in the sixteenth century, the route to Lough Derg reveals the remains of many monasteries and sites that would have been stations for the pilgrim, many with their own attractions. (These will be detailed below.)

7. RELICS: Christian pilgrimage is built upon visiting the relics of the saints. Initially these included the remains of the Apostles and martyrs found in catacombs and cemeteries as well as objects associated with the life of Christ, such as a piece from the stable at Bethlehem. These are classified as first-class relics.

Second-class relics are objects sanctified by having touched or been used by a saint, like St. Martin's Cloak, which was revered at Marmoutier Abbey at Tours, a stop along the route through France to

Santiago de Compostela. There are also third-class relics, which are small pieces of cloth touched to a first- or second-class relic.

Early pilgrims from Ireland to Rome brought back for their churches first-class relics of the more usual type — a hair of the Virgin Mary or St. Martin's Ankle Bone — but there were also indigenous first-class relics found in the tomb shrines of the early Irish saints. Downpatrick, for example, is thought to have the remains of the three patron saints of Ireland: Patrick, Columcille and Brigid.

There were also important second-class Irish relics, like St. Brigid's Shoe, but within this group there are also distinctly Irish relics. These were the bells, staffs and books of the early saints, which were usually encased in a protective and precious reliquary.

The following prescriptions from Irish penitential literature illustrate the significance of these staffs, bells (cymbals) and Gospel books, which were kept securely in the monasteries and used for ritual purposes, provided income and drew pilgrims.

> 1. If anyone in any way breaks into the place of keeping of the chrismal [i.e., a cloth used for covering the relics] of any saint, or a place of keeping for staves or cymbals, or takes away anything by robbery, or in any way injures a man, he shall make sevenfold restitution and remain through five years in hard penance on pilgrimage abroad. And if his penance is commendable, let him afterwards come to his own country; but if not, let him remain in perpetual exile.

> 2. If anyone breaks into the place of keeping of a Gospel book or removes anything by robbery, he

shall make sevenfold restitution, on account of the sevenfold grace of Christ and on account of the seven ecclesiastical ranks but he shall also remain through seven years in hard penance on pilgrimage. But if he does not do penance he is to be excommunicated from the whole Catholic Church and from the communion of all Christians, and burial in holy ground is not to be accorded to him.

Irish Canons from a Worcester Collection, c. 1000

The Itinerary (pp. 49–154, below) lists examples of these exclusively Irish relics and reliquaries, as well as others that have been identified along this route to Lough Derg. Many have been moved to museums, and their present location is noted. Many more have been lost or are presently unaccounted for.

8. EMBLEMS/TOKENS/MEMENTOS: Pilgrims badges or tokens were collected at pilgrimage sites as reminders and confirmations of the journey. Even today most shops at shrines sell a unique pin as souvenir — much like the badges that climbers collect for the mountains they've scaled. Pilgrim mementos were usually inexpensive or even free. The scallop shell, which could be collected from the shore of Galicia, is well recognized as the emblem of the pilgrimage to Santiago de Compostela and became a universal emblem for pilgrims in the Middle Ages.

At Station Island a "penal" crucifix was often brought away as a memento of the journey and, from their careful preservation, we know that they would often become important family heirlooms. These are very particular, well-documented, locally carved wooden objects that fit in the palm of a hand (Lucas, 1954). They are easily datable, since they have the year of the pilgrimage carved on the back. Examples survive from as early as 1702 and are still available, although today made in County Tyrone from peat or turf and without a date.

There are also two medieval references to a hand-held cross at Station Island, so the tradition probably long predates the surviving artifacts. In one pilgrimage account from 1353, we read how before George Grissaphan, a knight of Hungary, entered the purgatory the prior "placed the Cross of St. Patrick of great splendor and price in the left hand of George and fastened it with a cord as strongly as he could" (Leslie, 19). Antonio Mannini (1411) is also given a cross, which he is to bear in his right hand into the purgatory (Picard, 184).

In the Basilica of St. Patrick on Station Island there is currently a modern reliquary of the True Cross. However, in the Middle Ages there was evidently also a relic from the Cross. We know that in 1411 Laurence Rathold entered the cave with "round his neck...four pieces of the wood of the Holy Cross bound with snippets of the three tunics of Jesus Christ...as well as other precious relics."

9. RITES AND RITUALS: Pilgrimage itself is a ritual that may or should lead to an ecstatic experience — a stepping out of ordinary life, out of ordinary time — in order to arrive at a deeper understanding of the self and its place in the world (Turner, 1–39).

Pilgrimage also comprises certain rituals that give the pilgrim the opportunity to partake of the sacraments and participate in rites and prayers that culminate with the promised rewards of the journey. These rituals are an external and dramatic manifestation of the spiritual experience of pilgrimage and provide the opportunity for the community to recognize and solemnize the pilgrim's achievement.

In Rome, for instance, by the early thirteenth century, pilgrims were enjoined to visit the stational churches, in each of which the pope would say Mass on an appointed day — usually during the 40 days of Lent. At the end of this round of ceremonial church-going the promised indulgences would be conferred on the pilgrims who successfully completed all the requirements.

The pilgrimage at St. Patrick's Purgatory once involved long rituals of prayer and fasting before a pilgrim was permitted to spend a night in the cave on Station Island. After the cave was closed in the seventeenth century, fasting and prayers and the rounds of the penitential beds have remained integral parts of this pilgrimage ritual.

10. MOTIVATIONS — PENANCE AND PETITIONS: The motives for undertaking pilgrimage most often involve penance for a past act or petition for a future blessing. Pilgrimage was often juridically sanctioned as a punishment for a crime or penance for a sin (pp. 21–23, below). For instance, Peter Damian, the eleventh-century reformer and saint, sent corrupt

clergy on pilgrimage to Rome and Santiago. From the earliest account (c.1185) of the Knight Owein, the pilgrimage to St. Patrick's Purgatory was embarked upon to atone for sins. George Grissaphan (1353) visited Lough Derg to atone for crimes that he committed as a knight. More than any other site, Lough Derg is, by its very nature, associated with penance.

Often the blessing pilgrims sought would be salvation in the next life, sometimes for themselves, but sometimes for a loved one. Pilgrims have always prayed for cures for themselves and for others from the physical and spiritual woes of this life. Particularly at St. Patrick's Purgatory, however, some pilgrims came seeking visions of the otherworld.

11. EXPECTATIONS — INDULGENCES AND MIRACLES: The remission of sins and cancellation of their associated punishments through indulgences were considered among the most essential outcomes of pilgrimage. Gerald of Wales (c.1200) visited Rome as a pilgrim and amassed 92 years of indulgences after attending 395 masses. Simone Sigoli (1384), Arnold von Harff (1496–99), and the 15th-century *Information for Pilgrims* include detailed listings of indulgences available in the Holy Land.

Many early texts assert that if anyone endures St. Patrick's Purgatory in a spirit of penance he will never suffer the pains of hell. A document of 12 August 1507 by Master Donatus Magrahe, prior of St. Patrick's Purgatory, mentions a share "in all the indulgences of divers Roman pontiffs and other bishops, namely 10,670 years granted to our place...." Even today a popular legend claims that three visits to Lough Derg will save any pilgrim from hell.

Indulgences are easier to grant than miracles. The prior could assure the pilgrim that all sins were expiated and forgiven, and all penances were dispatched. But the pilgrim seeking a particular miracle, including a vision of the otherworld, was not so easily satisfied, and many would have departed still expecting some blessing, or resigned by the ordeal of pilgrimage to the status quo, or perhaps, like the notorious monk of Eymstadt, disappointed.

12. EARLY RECORD: The major medieval pilgrimages are all well documented. Records for Jerusalem are the oldest, with the earliest dating to the fourth century; the earliest records for Rome date from the eighth century; while the earliest records for both St. Patrick's Purgatory and Santiago de Compostela date from the twelfth century. Since these documents refer to already existing sites, rituals and routes, we know that the pilgrimages predate the earliest surviving records.

13. LITERARY TRADITION: The major pilgrimage sites are documented through extensive writings, both personal accounts and guidebooks, and through other, direct and indirect, literary evidence.

Pilgrimage to Rome is documented by famous texts like the *Einseideln Itinerary* of the late eighth/

early nithth century; two *Mirabilia urbis Romae,* one from the twelfth century by Benedict and one from the late twelfth or early thirteenth century by Gregory; and the *Graphia aureae urbis Romae* of the thirteenth or fourteenth century. Over thirty accounts dating from the fourth to the fifteenth century document the pilgrimage to Jerulsaem. During the nineteenth century the Palestine Pilgrims Text Society published thirteen volumes of works concerning the pilgrimage to the Holy Land. The route to Compostela also engendered several important texts. (See also p. 23 below.)

For St. Patrick's Purgatory, Shane Leslie (xxxvii-xxxix) lists approximately 35 descriptive texts from before 1600, plus approximately 41 documents relating to the Purgatory from before 1700.

14. CULTURAL MEMORY: One of the more interesting developments in historical methodology today, borrowed from the insights of folklore, anthropology and sociology, is the attempt to establish and study cultural memory. Different from legend or oral tradition, it may include elements of both, but relies on the deep diachronic structures of place and social commentary to go beyond — but not against —verbal and visual documents.

Beyond the documentary records, and beyond the structures and signposts, the memory of pilgrimage sites and routes may survive and flourish in individual pilgrims and communities of pilgrims, and be preserved and transmitted outside conventional modes. Sometimes cultural memory may take form as object, like mementos or simple markings scratched in stone, and as rituals, like the customary pilgrimage practices of walking, fasting and prayer; or it may remain simply formless as a continuing but also changing knowledge — not a knowledge "about," but a knowledge "of," which the pilgrim experiences directly (Fentress and Wickham, 3; Geary, 1994, 9–16).

Before the churches were built and the documents written, a cultural memory about sacred objects and locations endured, allowing them to be identified long after the events that made them important. For instance, the memories of the tombs of Peter and Christ were preserved for three centuries before the official structures and documented rituals were established around them. These are revered places with a significance and memory beyond their existence in space. Similarly, the way to Lough Derg and the rituals of the place were remembered by individuals and communities, who shared and evolved them without the aid of written documents.

❖

This taxonomy can be applied to any pilgrimage destination, but the accompanying chart in Appendix 1 (pp. 155–63, below) compares Lough Derg with Rome, Santiago de Compostela and Jerusalem on these fourteen specific points, indicating how the Pilgrim's Way to St. Patrick's Purgatory fits within this taxonomy of medieval pilgrimage sites and routes.

Bell Tower above the now-overgrown entrance
to St. Patrick's Purgatory, Station Island.

CHAPTER 3.
PILGRIMS AND PILGRIMS' STORIES

CHRISTIAN PILGRIMS

From at least as early as the beginning of the fourth century, Christians — of all races and both genders — began to participate in the culture of pilgrimage. Some of the earliest pilgrims to the Holy Land were women, and there are early indications of African Christians making their way to Rome and certainly to the Holy Land; the noble, wealthy and powerful made their way to the shrines, as did the destitute and indigent; all seeking a connection to the sacred and forgiveness for sins.

Today people follow pilgrims' itineraries for a variety of reasons: spiritual, cultural and recreational. The motives for going on pilgrimage in the Middle Ages were perhaps narrower and confined more to the spiritual realm. As always, some traveled for gain and adventure of a more mundane type. But even within those parameters, clearly some went on pilgrimage to follow the path to perfection while, at the other extreme, some were sent on pilgrimage to atone for sins and crimes.

PENITENTIAL LITERATURE

The Irish penitential literature provides a good insight into the latter motivation. These works, the earliest of which dates from the mid-fifth century, provide elaborate lists of the penances for sins. The *Senchús*

Mor of c.445 advises pilgrimage for bishops who lie, steal or commit adultery, while the eighth-century *Collectio canonum Hibernensis* would, ironically, send them on pilgrimage for excessive absence from their office.

Other penitentials recommend pilgrimage for those who fornicate with their mothers, god-daughters and god-sisters; and also for those who commit adultery and as a result beget children. The *St. Hubert Penitential* of c.850 enjoins both the fornicator and his god-daughter or god-sister to pilgrimage for adultery. Stealing from a church and violating relics are also punishable in this way, as is murder, intentional or unintentional.

The *Old Irish Penitential* of c.800 advises exile in destitution for murder in anger, but allows the exception that pious anchorites can grant remission of this penance. Clearly then St. Patrick's Purgatory, with its community of anchoritic men, would be a destination for a penitent pilgrim seeking absolution. This may be the source of the often-repeated indulgence associated with St. Patrick's Purgatory: if a pilgrim endures the rituals of this place in a spirit of penance, he will never suffer the pains of hell.

This "exile" as it was also called, could be for a few months or it could be perpetual. The most usual terms were 3, 7 or 10 years. For Irish clerics, it is unclear whether exile would be from their monastery or from their kingdom, of which there were then five in Ireland. In either case, many Irish pilgrims could easily remain in Hibernia for lesser terms, but it is also quite possible that they left for Continental destinations.

While the penitentials have always been a controversial literature, with continuing questions about the texts and their purpose, it is clear that they were also influential, spreading beyond the Celtic and Anglo-Saxon areas into continental Europe and eventually becoming incorporated into canon law.

PILGRIMS TO LOUGH DERG

Compared to other major Christian pilgrimage routes and sites from the Middle Ages — Rome, Jerusalem, Santiago de Compostela — there is no shortage of pilgrims' accounts of the journey to, and experience at, St. Patrick's Purgatory. One list of pilgrimage accounts and itineraries for Jerusalem includes about 90 texts; for Rome there are many fewer, only about 14; for Compostela still fewer, about 10 (Davidson, passim; see also, pp. 17–18 above). But these numbers are just for comparison, because it is clear that many texts have been lost, some are not yet identified, and if identified, many remain unedited and untranslated, so they have not appeared in surveys on pilgrimage.

The same is true for Lough Derg: a great deal more manuscript research would need to be done before we would have a clear picture of the number of descriptions that have survived. One disadvantage for Lough Derg is that any documents that were on site were destroyed long ago. This is probably also true for other Irish, as well as Scottish and English, sacred sites.

If we focus solely on the medieval documents that have already been edited and translated, we still have a considerable number of texts when compared with the other sites. Few of these texts describe the actual journey in detail, preferring to focus on the particulars of gaining permission to visit the cave or of other experiences at the destination. Shane Leslie lists approximately 35 descriptive texts from before 1600, plus approximately 41 more documents relating to the Purgatory from before 1700.

Some descriptions are clearly based on others, essentially rewriting earlier texts, but the same is true for descriptions of Rome and Jerusalem as well. Like those descriptions, the Lough Derg accounts were not by local people — by Irish visitors only — but by travelers from England, France, Spain, Italy, Hungary, the Low Countries and Switzerland.

INDIVIDUAL PILGRIM ACCOUNTS

One pilgrim, the Knight Owein, traveled to Ireland and visited St. Patrick's Purgatory c.1146/7. Although he may be a fictional pilgrim, his experience was recorded by H. of Saltrey, a Cistercian monk, c.1185. This is perhaps the most famous of the Lough Derg narratives: the *Tractatus de Purgatorio Sancti Patricii*. Owein's guilt about his life as a knight led him to this pilgrimage destination to endure penance for the remission of his sins especially, according to Matthew Paris's account, of arson, rapine and pillaging churches. He is followed

c.1170 by an anonymous knight first recorded by
Peter of Cornwall c.1200.

George Grissaphan (Crissapan), a knight of
Hungary who took part in the invasion of Naples with
King Lewis in 1347/8, was responsible for from 250
to over 350 murders in that war before he reached the
age of 24. He traveled from Apulia to Avignon to seek
forgiveness for his sins. He then walked from there to
Santiago de Compostela, where he spent five months
nearby as a hermit at Santa Maria Finistierra. While
in Galicia he learned of St. Patrick's Purgatory, and
he walked through all of Gascony, Navarre, France
and England until he reached Ireland and finally St.
Patrick's Purgatory in 1353.

Another pilgrim, Ramon de Perellós, who had
been in the service of the pope at Avignon, traveled
to St. Patrick's Purgatory in 1397.

Guillebert de Lannoy, a chamberlain to the duke
of Burgundy and knight of the Golden Fleece, often
traveled on diplomatic missions. In 1421 he was
sent to Palestine by Henry V of England to gather
information for a possible crusade. In his report, the
Survey of Egypt, he makes some mention of Jerusalem
and the church of the Holy Sepulchre, but his work
is essentially a topographical and statistical account.
While in Scotland nine years later (1430), he detoured
to visit St. Patrick's Purgatory and left a description of
the route that forms the basis for the itinerary outlined
here in *The Pilgrim's Way to St. Patrick's Purgatory.*

The nature of his profession as diplomat —
perhaps even as spy — means that his attention to

topographical detail surpasses that of most other pilgrims, but is still not as thorough as we could have hoped. He measures, counts and provides orientations, but when he visits ancient churches and abbeys he pronounces them too poor to bother identifying. He is, of course, familiar with churches like Auxerre and monasteries like Cîteaux — no wonder he is unimpressed by these simple rural structures. Here is his account of the journey:

> Took sea May 27 to pass to Ireland and descended at Drogheda a walled town, three leagues by the sea on the River Boyne. Thence to Kennelich an ill-walled town still belonging to the King of England, seated on the frontier of the wild Irish. There is a poor Abbey. Thence rode to Canaen [Kennanus, Kells] a poor unwalled town belonging to King Auraly [O'Reilly] who lives in a wretched place and poor tower over the town. Passed to Coloniensy [Clonosey], a small village, went on foot into the forest because no horse could pass the fallen trees. Thence as far as a great lake where the lordship of King Auraly yields to the lordship and land of King Maguir and contains this lake 160 miles long and about 30 broad and in this lake they say there are 160 islands and this lake debuches into the North West sea. Went to a village and island called Rousseauxmoustier [Enniskillen] and all the houses are of wattles. It belongs to a Duke who has 1500 boats called Macanienus subject to the King Maguir. This Duke lent us a ship to go to St. Patrick's Hole. Passed by several islands where we disembarked to dine and sleep. For their poverty I will not mention them. Found ancient little Churches and poor Abbeys. From this lake to St. Patrick's lake there are four miles by land. We left there our ship

and went the four miles on foot. Passed as far as the Isle of St. Patrick's Purgatory, which is half a mile in another ship. (Leslie, 39.)

An 1878 edition of Lannoy's Travels (Lannoy, 169), identifies "Kennelich" as "Kells" and reads "Canaen" as "Cavaen," identifying it as "Cavan." At Clonosey, about 10 k (6 mi) northeast of Drumlane, there is record of a hospital, probably at the location marked on old maps as "friary ruins," but now without any remains.

Other medieval pilgrims include Nicholas, a nobleman, seeking to do penance; and the Sire of Beaujeau (before 1352); Taddeo Gualandi of Pisa (before 1359); Louis d'Auxerre (French) and a certain Malatesta de Rimini and Nicholas Beccari of Ferrara (both Italian), (all 1358); Guido Cissi (Italian) and John Bonham (English), (both 1365); Sir William Lisle, a knight of King Richard II, and another English knight (1394–95); William "Lord of Corsy" (English/ French, 1397); John of Brederode (1399); a German monk of the order of St. Bernard (1400); William of Stranton (English, 1409); Antonio da Focha (ante-1411); Laurence Rathold of Pászthó, a Hungarian knight, and Antonio Mannini, a Florentine merchant (1411); Eugene O'Brien of England (ante-1412); Conrad von Scharnachthal (Swiss, 1446); Sir John de Banste (Flemish, 1460); Jean Garry, François Proty and Jean Burgey (French, 1485); John Bermyngham and William Bramery (English, 1489); Blasius Biragus (ante-1494); Nylanus O'Ledan (Irish, 1507); an anonymous French knight (1516); and Guarino of Durazzo (Italian, ante-1518).

The papal nuncio Francesco Chiericati, who in 1522 represented Pope Adrian VI at the Diet of Nuremberg, charged with carrying out previous judgments against Martin Luther, had been a visitor to Lough Derg in 1517. While two of his companions entered the Purgatory, he did not, but apparently spent his time examining the records on this island. He reports that he saw a book, now lost, that recorded the names of previous pilgrims.

However, in 1494, before Chiericati arrived, a Dutch Augustinian canon from Eymstadt, the notorious "monk of Eymstadt," visited the cave, was sorely disappointed by his experience and petitioned Pope Alexander VI to close the cave and thus put an end to the simonistic practices that the canon found there, noting that he had refused repeatedly to pay anything to bishop, prince or prior.

Curiously, the cave that this canon describes in no way corresponds to the cave that the other pilgrims describe over the course of several centuries. He claims that the sacristan lowered him down on a rope into a pit — and lowered down some bread and a flask of water — then hauled him up again the next morning. No other texts mention sacristans or ropes or sustenance as part of the ritual, nor especially being lowered into a pit.

According to the only surviving account of this incident, which is not a primary document (Haren, 190–92), the pope ordered that the place of fallacy be destroyed, but it is unclear whether the documents describe one or two places. Is the place where "the Purgatory once was," the same as "the site of fallacy"? Although something was indeed closed up at this time, perhaps it was not the cave all the other pilgrims describe, but the place of fallacy — the hole that the monk was lowered into, perhaps as a joke played on him by the island's canons in revenge for his niggardliness.

The *Annals of Ulster* for 1497 seem to confirm that the place closed was not the real St. Patrick's Purgatory, but a false one. It records that "The cave of Patrick's Purgatory in Lough Gerg was destroyed about the festival of St. Patrick this year, by the guardian of Donegal and by the representative of the bishop in the deanery of Lough Erne [i.e., Cathal Maguire], by authority of the pope, the people in general having understood from the history of the knight [Owein], and other old books, that this was not the Purgatory which St. Patrick obtained from God, though the people in general were visiting it."

In any case, there is clear evidence that within about twenty years the site was still (or again) welcoming pilgrims. It was officially suppressed in 1632 and everything on the island destroyed, although apparently the actual owner of the property permitted the canons to remain.

Another papal nuncio, Giovanni Battista Rinnucinni, attempted to reestablish the Purgatory in 1648 during the Irish Confederate Wars, but this failed, as did much of his mission in Ireland. Yet it seems the pilgrimage still continued: in 1700, 5,000 pilgrims were recorded for the season; in 1701 fewer than 2,000 were counted by August 1, but on this day alone there were 300 on the island. Starting in 1710 the Franciscans would repair to the lake every year to counsel the pilgrims, even though as of 1763 they had still not built a permanent residence there. By 1826 the number of pilgrims grew to 15,000, and to 30,000 by 1846, just before the onset of the Great Famine. From 1871 to 1903 approximately 3,000 pilgrims visited annually; and from 1908 to 1921, the number averaged over 8,000. From 1929 to the end of the century the number never fell below 10,000 pilgrims, and in many years was twice, and sometimes thrice, that number.

The site now attracts about 30,000 pilgrims each year during the main part of the pilgrimage season from early June until August 15, and pilgrims continued to write about their experiences, including well-known poets, such as Denis Devlin, Patrick Kavanagh and Seamus Heaney; and others, including Pete McCarthy, a famous TV presenter.

CHAPTER 4. MEDIEVAL ROADS AND MODERN ROUTES

INTRODUCTION

Medieval pilgrimage, while essentially spiritual, is also heavily entwined with topography and landscape. It is, in fact, the place where devotion and geography intersect. Unusual physical places, like mountain tops, natural caves and springs, often assume a sacred quality, and extraordinary events, such as miracles and visions, are linked to them, marking them as sacred spaces. St. Patrick's Purgatory and the route there weave together Ireland's sacred legacy with its landscape and geography.

Old maps and itineraries are important assets in reconstructing historical routes, as work in the field of historical geography has demonstrated. *The Pilgrim's Way to St. Patrick's Purgatory* was sketched out from a pilgrim's itinerary of 1430. Guillebert de Lannoy's account is sometimes vague and uncertain, but it does lay out a particular direction. Although many pilgrims started from Dublin, he started farther along at Drogheda and stopped at Kells, Cavan, Clonosey, Enniskillen and on islands in Lough Erne. In his account we discern the pattern of a traveler moving up the Boyne Valley into the Blackwater Valley and then into the lake system that feeds into and becomes Lough Erne.

We also know that pilgrims did not invent their own paths, but relied on the usual roads used for trade and travel. In sparsely populated, rural lands

Betelius' Map of Ireland, 1560.

like Ireland, the roads did not change much into the nineteenth century, and from historical maps we can still identify the old routes — the Dublin Roads — that would have formed the main thoroughfares across the landscape. Some old roads still maintain the names of the towns and sites that they connected: Old Mellifont Road, Kells Road, Oldcastle Road, etc. Until the twentieth century when the N3s and the M2s were needed to accommodate the automobile, many of these roads remained intact, and often the new routes were built on top of the old roads: the N3 from Navan to Kells is just one example.

European maps (Italian, German, English and Dutch) from as early as the fifteenth century show very few towns in Ireland, but many locate St. Patrick's Purgatory appropriately in the northwestern corner. By the time that detailed maps of Ireland do appear, many of the monasteries — the likely stopping places of pilgrims — would already have been destroyed in the sixteenth and seventeenth centuries, leaving only ruins, which were indeed sometimes recorded on nineteenth-century maps.

St. Patrick's Purgatory and Lough Derg continue to appear on Irish maps from the sixteenth to the eighteenth centuries, which also include towns along the route like Swords, Lusk, Drogheda, Mellifont, Slane, Navan, Kells, Oldcastle and Kilmore. A map printed in London in 1712 (Senex & Marshall) includes every town along this route from Dublin to Pettigo, as well as the abbeys Castlekeeran, Drumlane, Derrybrusk, Lisgoole and Inishmacsaint. On maps from the 1820s through the 1840s, it is quite possible to trace the old routes that would have survived from earlier periods, passing through these towns and past the ruins on our itinerary.

MEDIEVAL ACCOUNTS OF THE ROUTE

As we have already noted, the route we have laid our derives mainly from the description left by one fifteenth-century pilgrim, Guillebert de Lannoy. Of the many pilgrims who made the trip each year, virtually none left any written record. Of those who did — and those who wrote from second-hand knowledge — far fewer left any account of their journey as far as Lough Derg, many just picking up from the point of their arrival there.

Old Mellifont Road.

Of the eight reports on the journey, one mentions simply how long it took: John of Brederode (1399) left the Low Countries during Lent, between February 17th and March 29th, and returned June 12th, taking at minimum two and a half months.

Two others only sketch the route as far as Ireland, even failing to make mention of their landing spot: in 1353 George Grissaphan reports that he walked through Gascony in southwest France and Navarre in northeast Spain — surely in reverse order — then all of France, England and Ireland; and in 1446 Conrad von Scharnachthal reports that he traveled to Ireland from Scotland.

Antonio Mannini, who made the pilgrimage in 1411 with Laurence Rathold of Pászthó, mentions that they started in Dublin on September 25th and traveled for three and a half months for the round trip. Rathold does not mention any details of the route, but he made it clear that he had wider horizons than simply the ultimate destination, since he writes that he wants to see "the marvels and miracles of the saints of Ireland, for I had heard much of these marvels and miracles, the great diversity of which I had learned from many sources."

Two travelers mention getting as far as Lough Derg and being sent away to Armagh to get letters of permission to enter the cave: George Grissaphan (1353) and the notorious monk of Eymstadt (1494). The former is also obliged to get a letter from the bishop of Clogher, and the trip to Armagh and back takes him eight days. It is possible to posit from this

that neither initially passed through Armagh on their
way to Lough Derg, because most likely they would
then have been aware of the need for letters.

Three accounts — Peter of Cornwall's second-
hand report from 1200, Ramon de Perellós' of 1397
and Francesco Chiericati's of 1517 — speak of a
route through Armagh. Peter says that it's a four-day
journey from Dublin, through Mellifont, St. Patrick's
Monastery (probably Newry) and Armagh to Lough
Derg. Ramon, who leaves the papal court at Avignon
on Sept. 6, 1397, proceeds from Dublin, through
Drogheda, Dundalk and Armagh. And Chiericati,
passing through Chester in England and arriving in
Dublin, travels through Dromore, Dundalk, Armagh,
and Omagh; returning through Armagh, Newry and
Downpatrick, back to Dublin.

Topographically, however, the Armagh route had a
particular disadvantage since both south and west of
that city the terrain is quite hilly, even mountainous.
These late medieval travelers were more than pilgrims
and apparently had business in Armagh that most,
more humble, medieval pilgrims did not. Some late
medieval travelers may also have considered it an
advantage that much of this route was under English
control during this period.

The important report of Guillebert de Lannoy
of 1430 presents a full picture of a quite different
route. Lannoy was a well informed and profesional
traveler. He would therefore, most likely, have taken
the most widely accepted and accessible route; and
his testimony carries great authority.

He begins in Drogheda and mentions passing though Kennelich [an ill-walled town in English hands, which is identified by a later editor as Kells], Canaen or Cavaen [identified by different editors alternately as Kells or Cavan], Coloniensy [Clonosey], and Rousseauxmoustier [Enniskillen]. He then mentions that the duke there lent him and his companions a boat so they could travel up Lough Erne and that they stopped at several islands to eat and sleep on their way to the northern shore. Although there are many islands in Lough Erne, few of them are excavated (Cunningham, 2000), but Devenish, Inishmacsaint and White Island are rich repositories of medieval pilgrimage culture. Once Lannoy reaches the northern shore he mentions traveling another four miles by foot before embarking on another boat to take him a half mile to Station Island, or as he calls it, St. Patrick's Hole. For the historical, cultural, topographical and practical reasons laid out below, Lannoy's account, which appears the most complete and authoritative, is the basis of our Pilgrim's Way.

THE MEDIEVAL TRAVELERS
AND THEIR CHOICES:
LITERAL EVIDENCE

Without doubt, the types of people who made the pilgrimage to Lough Derg throughout the Middle Ages varied considerably. It would be safe to acknowledge that the records we do have come from a very special type of pilgrim. Of the four full accounts, those of Ramon de Perellós (1397), Guillebert de Lannoy (1430) and Francesco Chiericati (1517) are first-hand. These are all literate men of wealth and power: the first straight from the court of the pope at Avignon, the second an agent of the duke of Burgundy and the king of England, and the third the papal nuncio to England.

Guillebert de Lannoy traveled by horse, but at Clonosey, near Drumlane, the thick forest forced him to proceed on foot. He had been on embassy as far as Scotland, and we also know that he had been sent to the Holy Land to assess and report on the lay of the land pending a new crusade. Is he spying out the Irish parts of Ireland for the English on this trip? He does not specifically say, but he was certainly used to diplomatic correspondence of a certain type and it is interesting to note that certain habits of this type of reporting linger in his account: he mentions particularly the kings of each area — something that is left unmentioned by all others — whether a town is walled, the border on the region with the "wild" Irish, the number of boats belonging to the duke at Enniskillen and the building materials used in different places. He gives distances and dimensions, but mostly he finds an impoverished place hardly worth his attention.

Ramon de Perellós and Francesco Chiericati, on the other hand, traveled via Armagh, the seat of the primate in Ireland. This is a more difficult landscape — hilly, even mountainous, with far fewer monasteries for hospitality — but these are men traveling in retinue on horses, and if they do not mention specifically that they are on official business, they are traveling to places where they are likely to meet, or specifically visit, their own colleagues and associates.

Even Peter of Cornwall's second-hand description contextualizes the route in terms of individual monks and bishops and their relationship to institutions in Dublin, Mellifont, Newry and Armagh. While these may be pilgrims, they are also business travelers. In fact, Chiericati, unlike Guillebert, never even enters the cave, but prefers to examine the documents at Lough Derg while two of his companions participate in that ritual.

PHYSICAL EVIDENCE

Most likely because of their social and economic status, we are missing literary accounts of travelers on foot. But from physical and archaeological evidence we know that pilgrims traveled through this region. We have one clear, first-hand pilgrim account, evidence of relics and tombs of important Irish saints and the remains of monastic establishments closely strung together where pilgrims could find hospitality. We also have the acknowledged significance of pilgrimage as a practice throughout Ireland, and specifically along this route.

This evidence indicates that this was a journey that normally took several months. Even allowing a month at Lough Derg for 15 days of fasting and penance before and after a night in the purgatorial cave — the longest recorded duration — these, in general, were not trips made in four days on horseback, but more likely about 15 days walking approximately 218 k (140 mi) in one direction — durations that would be in keeping with assigned penances of months or years of pilgrimage for crimes like murder and adultery.

ADVANTAGES OF THIS ROUTE

The advantages of this route, which would have been the same route as one used by both traders and travelers, are evident from a topographical map. The

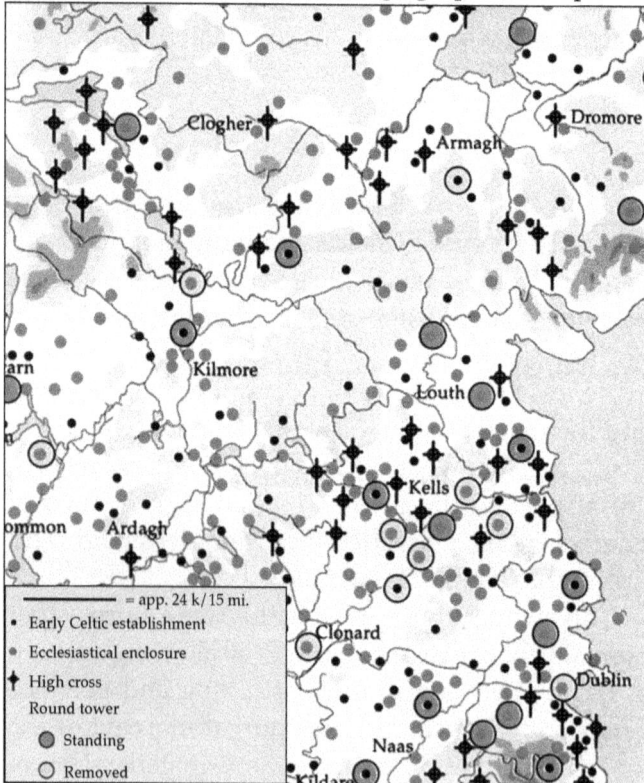

Early Christian Ecclesiastical Sites. From F.H.A. Aalen, et al., *Atlas of the Irish Rural Landscape*, 51.

route traverses the low lands along the coast, then turns inland at Drogheda and up the Boyne Valley, which is logical, indeed inherent, since this region has been a settlement area of Ireland since the third milennium B.C.E. The route then moves into the Blackwater Valley, avoiding higher lands on either side. After Kells it sidesteps Slieve na Calliagh, the highest peak in Meath, by passing east of it, then follows close by the eastern edge of Lough Sheelin. Around Kilmore it enters the system of lakes and rivers that eventually feeds into Lough Erne, avoiding the hills and mountains to the east and west.

A map of early Christian ecclesiastical sites shows a marked density of establishments, enclosures, round towers and high crosses along this same route compared with the surrounding areas. This is clearly evident in the region of the Boyne and Blackwater Valleys. The area around Kilmore and Drumlane with seven enclosures, four establishments, two round towers and a high cross within an area of about 400 sq. k. (c. 150 sq. mi.), is on the average greater than ten times as dense as the surrounding areas to the east and west with no more than one or two sites within the same expanse.

In addition to the advantages of, and medieval evidence for, this route, another advantage now is the survival of significant remains in this region. Considering how thoroughly destruction visited monastic establishments from the 1520s on, it is remarkable that so much does remain. Fortunately the Way is mostly through rural areas. Subsequently there was relatively little destruction of those few remains by modern improvements, such as major highways or housing and commercial development.

Except for one spot it is not at all difficult to link one place to another approximately every 20 k (12 mi) — the usual day's walk for a pilgrim along an established and well-traveled route, as any modern walker can attest. The Way takes the pilgrim through a remarkable landscape of round towers, high crosses and monastic ruins of significant importance and great beauty, making it a pilgrim's way that follows the contours of the land and the past.

ALTERNATE ROUTES

As we know from our taxonomy of pilgrimage (pp. 5–19, above), there is always more than one route to a pilgrimage site. There has always been more than one route to Rome, even though the Via Francigena is now the route of choice for modern pilgrims.

A trip to the Holy Land could begin at almost any Mediterranean port, from Barcelona to Brindisi and Venice to Constantinople; it could even be an overland journey.

There are also several ways to approach Santiago de Compostela, depending on the starting point and probably influenced as well by weather, season and political circumstances. The primary route has, however, become an archetypal cultural itinerary.

We already have discussed one alternate route to Lough Derg. There was also another — although a short one — from Donegal to Lough Derg, and

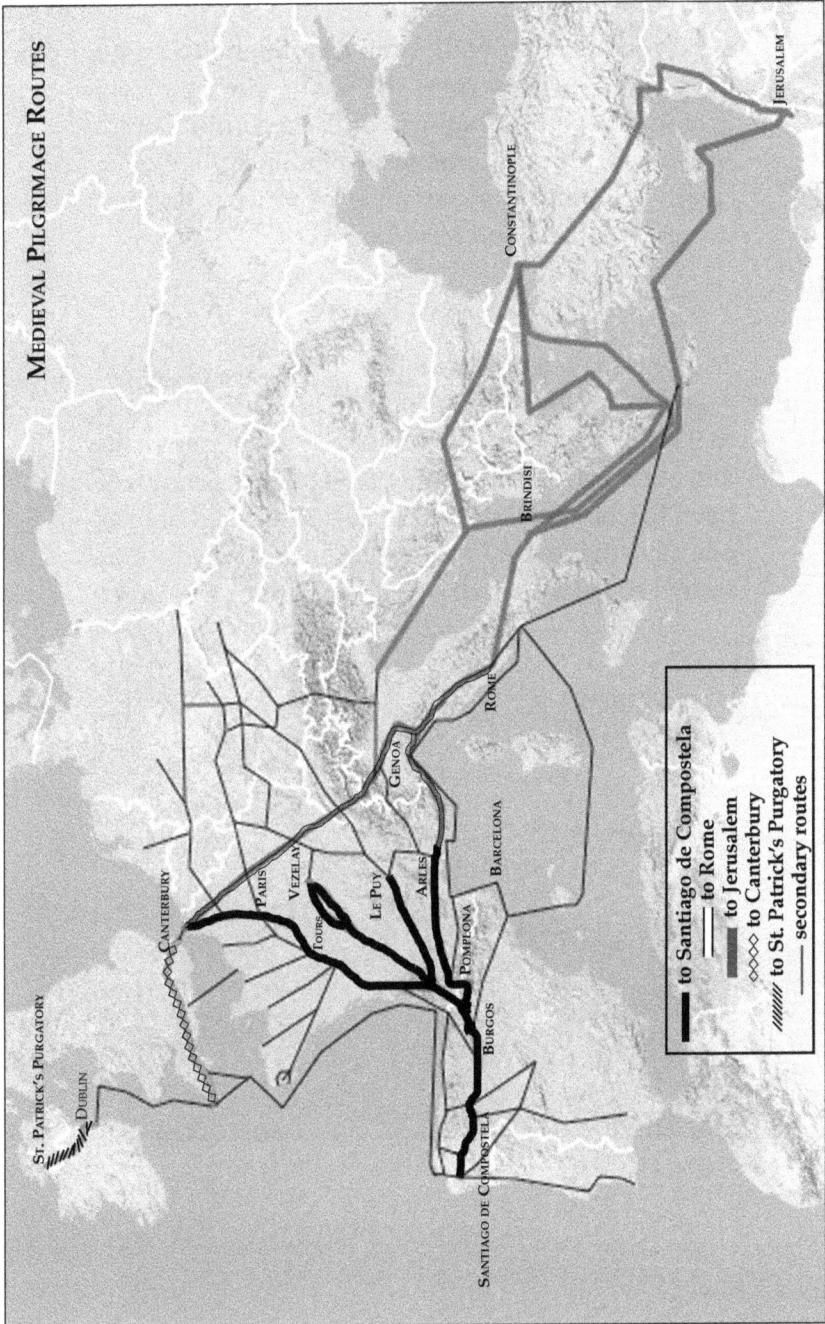

Medieval Pilgrimage Routes

to Santiago de Compostela
to Rome
to Jerusalem
◇◇◇ to Canterbury
///// to St. Patrick's Purgatory
secondary routes

St. Patrick's Purgatory
Dublin
Canterbury
Paris
Vezelay
Tours
Le Puy
Arles
Genoa
Pomplona
Burgos
Barcelona
Santiago de Compostela
Rome
Brindisi
Constantinople
Jerusalem

no doubt one as well that approached Lough Derg more directly from the south, perhaps from Limerick up the Shannon and then into Lough Erne. The proponderance of evidence, however, clearly indicates that our present route is the best documented and and traveled.

Links to Europe

The previous map shows how the medieval world was covered by an interlocking lacework of roads that were used by pilgrims as well as by merchants and other travelers. Several of the pilgrims known to have reached St. Patrick's Purgatory visited at least one other major site: Owein and Guillebert de Lannoy visited the Holy Land; Antonio Mannini, Francesco

St. Uny, Cornwall.

Chiericati and the monk of Eymstadt visited Rome, as did, no doubt, many others; George Grissaphan and Laurence Rathold visited Santiago de Compostela. We also have evidence that pilgrims left Ireland for Compostela on a regular basis. For instance, there was a hostel in Dublin, St. James of Compostela at the Steyne, for lepers on their way to the shrine in Galicia. In addition, the sculptural remains from the Lough Erne basin provide clear evidence of pilgrimage activity between this area and France and Spain (Wood, 47–48).

This map of medieval pilgrimage routes shows how these interconnected routes stretch as far south and east as Jerusalem and as far north and west as Donegal, including two routes of southwest Britain, St. Michael's Way and Saints' Way. The first crosses Cornwall at the far west, stretching from St. Michael's Mount near Penzance to St. Uny in Lelant, just east of St. Ives. This is an area associated with St. Erc from Slane, since he was the brother of both Sts. Uny and Ia (Ives), and a small village just south of St. Uny is named for Erc (St. Erth).

Saints' Way crosses Cornwall between Fowey and Padstow and has an array of Celtic saints associated with it: Petroc, Uvell (Eval), Ingungar (probably Congar) and Fimbarrus.

These routes across Cornwall avoided the often dangerous sea voyage around Land's End. From the south pilgrims could continue across the sea to Wales or Ireland and from the north either east overland to Canterbury and Dover or south by ship to France and Spain. George Grissaphan specifically mentions that he walked through England, after walking through Navarre, Gascony and France. Obviously he relied on few ships during his pilgrimage, and perhaps landed in England at Dover to visit Canterbury and London before proceeding west to Cornwall, perhaps stopping at pilgrimage sites along the entire way.

These individual routes constitute a transcontinental pilgrimage network, and we are now able to show it as stretching from Santiago de Compostela and Jerusalem to Canterbury, connecting to London, Plymouth, Dublin and on to St. Patrick's Purgatory.

Overview of the Modern Route

The Pilgrim's Way laid out here begins in Dublin and heads north through Swords and Lusk to Drogheda, where it turns west through the Boyne Valley as far as Donaghmore (Navan), passing first through Mellifont and Slane. The way then turns northwest to Kells and to a small outpost at Castlekeeran, then continues northwest to Kilmore and Drumlane. Here we enter the Lough Erne region: off the upper (southern) lake, we encounter Aghalurcher and in the lower (northern) lake: Devenish, Inishmacsaint and White Island, before arriving at Pettigo for the short journey north to Lough Derg.

Transportation

There are several ways to follow this pilgrimage route. The most obvious one is by automobile. Most people probably arrive at most pilgrimage sites today by car. It is the exceptional pilgrim who walks, bikes or sails. Walking and cycling are, however, very good choices for Ireland, and all these are possible ways to reach Lough Derg. The pilgrim can, of course, only travel part of the way by boat: from Drumlane, and certainly from Belturbet, the journey to just south of Pettigo could be made by boat along the Lough Erne Waterway, and there are several places where a boat is absolutely necessary: for Devenish, White Island, and Station Island.

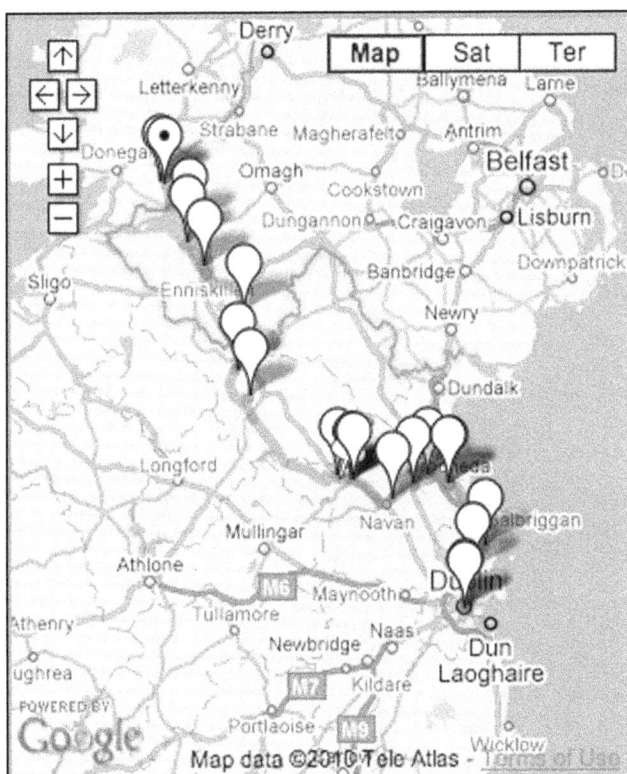

Although there is now no path for walkers only, the roads in this region of Ireland tend to be small and quiet. Picking the right time of the day and the week can help the walker avoid traffic. And there are probably many byways that have not yet been identified that can help the walker avoid automobile roads altogether.

In addition, Ireland has a good bus system, and from Dublin to Pettigo there is regular service. In summer there are buses directly to the Visitor Centre at Lough Derg. If traveling by bus, a good deal of walking might be required to reach places like Mellifont, Castlekeeran, Kilmore and Drumlane from the nearest stops. Nevertheless, it is a good alternative. Rail is more limited, but does make connections from Dublin to Lusk, and on to Drogheda.

CHAPTER 5.

ITINERARY

This itinerary presents the sixteen stations of the route from Dublin to Lough Derg. Each numbered section provides information on the following: maps (Ordnance Survey Discovery and Discoverer Series numbers), access, parking and amenities; the monuments, their remains and history and the saints and relics associated with the site; nearby points of interest; with web addresses for online resources, such as picture galleries, travelers resources and bibliographies. Each section is also accompanied by a detail map of the route.

1. DUBLIN

Map: OS 50

Amenities: As the major city of Ireland, there is nothing a pilgrim can't find here from an airport to youth hostels.

ST. PATRICK'S CATHEDRAL

History: Tradition holds that a well at this site was connected with St. Patrick and his mission to baptize the people of Dublin in the fifth century and that a wooden church was built at that time to honor his visit. Documentary evidence places a church here as early as 1121, and grave slabs suggest a foundation here of the tenth or eleventh century. The original

St. Patrick's Cathedral, Dublin.

establishment would have been on an island in the River Poddle, and hence the church was once named St. Patrick in Insula (on the Island). In 1192 a collegiate church built of stone was rededicated to God, the Blessed Virgin and St. Patrick. It became a cathedral in 1213; and a new church in the Gothic style of Salisbury was largely completed by 1254.

Remains: Six early-Christian grave slabs or cross stones. Two are reportedly built into the fabric of the church's roof space with four on display: two located at the western end of the north aisle and two in the south transept.

Of those in the north aisle, one from the ninth century, inscribed with a Latin and a Greek cross, was found during the 1901 excavations and formed

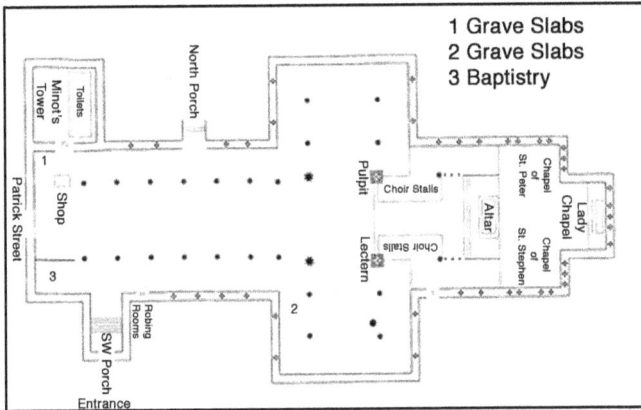

St. Patrick's Cathedral, floor plan.

part of the culvert for the River Poddle, apparently marking the site of St. Patrick's Well. The other slab has a two-line cross. The two crosses in the south transept have been dated to the seventh and tenth centuries, one with four crosses: a large Greek cross, a large Latin cross and two smaller Latin crosses; the other with two Latin crosses.

The baptistery, in the two western bays of the south aisle, at the entrance, is considered to be a remnant of the twelfth-century church, although the vaulting is later. Here there are medieval flooring tiles, re-laid from the south transept, and an undated medieval font.

Italica Picture Gallery:
http://gallery.me.com/egardiner#100222

Online references:
http://www.stpatrickscathedral.ie
http://two.archiseek.com/2010/1191-st-patricks-cathedral-patrick-street-dublin/

51

Bibliography:
Crawford & Gillespie.
Gwynn & Hadcock, 71–72.
Harbison (1992), 128–29.

Access: Open all year from 09:00 to 17:00 or 17:30, earlier closing on Sundays in winter. Admission fee charged.

Parking: There is no car parking on site.

Amenities: On site, there are toilets and a gift shop.

Route: St. Patrick's Cathedral to Christ Church Cathedral

Starting at St. Patrick's Cathedral, follow St. Patrick St. north into St. Nicholas St. into Winetavern St. Christ Church Cathedral will be on the left. (Approximately 0.5 k/0.3 mi.)

CHRIST CHURCH CATHEDRAL

History: The Church or Priory of the Holy Trinity, later known as Christ Church Cathedral, is associated with pilgrimage to Rome. It was founded c.1038 by

Christ Church Cathedral, Dublin.

Dunan, first bishop of Dublin. The first building was probably of wood, and there are no remains of it. The second is from the end of the eleventh century. Initially a Benedictine establishment, under St. Laurence O'Toole it was transferred to the Augustinian Canons from c.1163, and a new building was begun within the next decade. The existing transept was begun c.1175. The steeple, from 1283, the chapter house, dormitory and cloister were all destroyed by fire with further damage to the steeple in 1326 and 1461. In 1562 the nave vaulting collapsed, taking down the south wall and roof.

Remains: South of the present church are the remains of the long quire (fourteenth century) and the old chapter house (thirteenth century). The south transept doorway is from the 1180s. The Peace Chapel of St. Laud in the extreme southeast end of the cathedral incorporates the original medieval floor tiles that survived in 63 distinct patterns, including the famous "fox" pilgrim tile (although the original of this particular tile is not on view). These tiles were replicated during the Victorian restoration for use through the building.

Also here is the reliquary of the heart of St. Laurence O'Toole (d. 1180). The north and south transepts survive from the twelfth-century church. In the north transept and adjoining nave are Romanesque and Gothic stone capitals. Much of the present nave dates from the thirteenth century but is considerably restored. The crypt survives from the late twelfth-century construction.

Relics: This church boasted a rich collection of relics, including the renowned Speaking Crucifix and the Staff of Jesus, but all the relics, which attracted many pilgrims, were publicly burned in 1538.

Italica Picture Gallery:
http://gallery.me.com/egardiner#100229

Online references:
http://cccdub.ie/
http://two.archiseek.com/2010/1172-christ-church-cathedral-dublin/

Bibliography:
Gwynn & Hadcock, 170–71.
Harbison (1992), 125–26.

Access: Opens 09:45, except Sundays when it opens for visitors at 12:30; closing time is either 16:15 or 18:15, depending on the day and season. Admission charge.

Parking: None on site.

Amenities: On site there is a gift/book shop.

Nearby Points of Interest :
St. Mary's Abbey (Meetinghouse Lane off Capel St., north of the Liffey) is an important site on the pilgrimage route to Lough Derg. Unfortunately, at this time, access to its few remains (a chapter house and slype) are limited. Traditionally dated to the tenth century, but officially founded as a Benedictine house in 1139, it became the wealthiest Cistercian abbey in Ireland, after it was transferred to them by St. Malachy in 1147.

The abbey played an important role in both trade and travel from the Continent, and it maintained its own quay on the Liffey. Here ships from Bristol and beyond were frequent visitors, exporting the abbey's agricultural surplus and carrying pilgrims and other travelers.

The National Museum of Ireland — in addition to important permanent exhibitions on the history of Ireland, especially during the medieval period — houses one of the most important collections of Irish medieval relics, several of them associated with the pilgrimage to Lough Derg.

Trinity College Library houses one of the most important Irish relics of the Middle Ages and one of the best known relics associated with the pilgrimage to Lough Derg, the Book of Kells.

Dublinia is a heritage center on the Vikings and on medieval Dublin at Christ Church Cathedral. Its scale model of medieval Dublin is an important visual tool.

Route:
Dublin to Swords

Continue on Winetavern St. to the river and make a left onto Merchant's Quay. The next bridge on the right is the site of the original medieval bridge across the Liffey. A recommended stop north of the river is the remains of the great St. Mary's Abbey, but this is currently not easy to arrange. From here we follow Church St. into King St. N. and the N1 into Swords Rd. (R132), which becomes the Dublin Rd. (R127) at the Airport Roundabout. At the Pinnock Hill Roundabout the Dublin Rd. heads north (R132 again). This leads straight into Swords, where a left turn on Church Rd. brings the pilgrim to the first round tower of the journey. (Approximately 13 k/8.6 mi.)

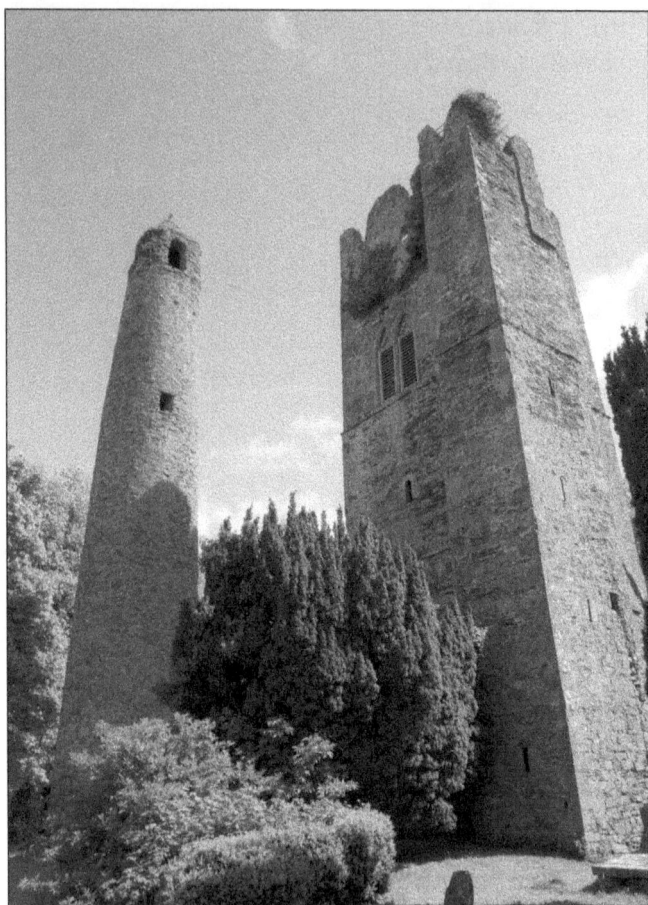

Round Tower with adjacent medieval tower, Swords.

2. SWORDS

History: A monastery (Sord-coluim-cille) was founded here by St. Columcille in the early sixth century. It was burned in 994, and burned and plundered several times between 1020 and 1166.

Remains: The round tower, which probably dates from the tenth century, is the only remnant of the early monastery. The tower is largely reconstructed. A door on the ground level faces east (the steps to the door are modern), and there are rectangular windows in the drum and four arched widows on the bell floor facing the cardinal points of the compass. These towers may have been used as look-outs, belfries or refuges, where people and precious goods were hidden during raids.

Saints:
ST. COLUMCILLE (pp. 82–83, below).

Italica Picture Gallery:
http://gallery.me.com/egardiner#100437

Online references:
http://roundtowers.org/swords/index.html
http://www.libraryireland.com/articles/
    RoundTowerSwordsDPJ1-23/index.php

Bibliography:
    Gwynn & Hadcock, 44.
    Harbison (1992), 136.
    Lalor, 140–41, 143.

Access: The site is under the stewardship of St. Columba's Church, Swords.

Map: OS 50

Parking: Across the road, opposite the church.

Amenities: Dublin Road–Dublin Street–Main Street, Swords has numerous pubs, restaurants and shops.

Route: Swords to Lusk

Continue on Church Rd. and make a right onto Bridge St. (R125). Follow R125 to the Estuary Roundabout, where you take the R127 north directly into Lusk. This small trip will bring the pilgrim to the second round tower, off the square in Lusk. (Approximately 9 k/5.6 mi.)

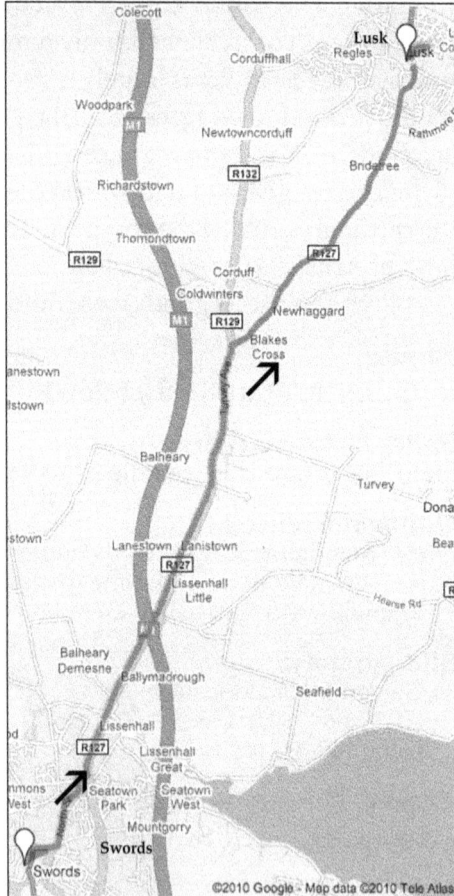

3. LUSK

History: A monastery was founded here by St. Mac Cuilinn (d. 496 or 498) at the end of the fifth century. It was plundered by Vikings in 827 and 856; in 1053;

Round Tower, Lusk.

in 1089 by the men of Munster; and in 1133 when the church full of people and its relics were burned by the men of Meath. A convent of Augustinian (Arrouaise) nuns, in Lusk from 1144 to 1195(?), was later transferred to Grace Dieu.

Remains: The round tower of the tenth or eleventh century was joined to the later belfry (of c.1500) with its three additional towers. It is the only remnant of the early monastery.

Saints:
St. Mac Cuilinn. (Also Cuindid, Cuindedha, Chuinnedha.)

Little is know about this saint, son of Cathbad, who founded a monastery at Lusk, except for the notation of his death on September 6, 496 (*Annals of Tigernach*)/498 (*Annals of Ulster*).

Italica Picture Gallery:
http://gallery.me.com/egardiner#100196

Online references:
http://en.wikipedia.org/wiki/Lusk,_County_Dublin
http://roundtowers.org/lusk/index.html
http://www.heritageireland.ie/en/midlandseastcoast/
   LuskHeritageCentre/

Bibliography:
Gwynn & Hadcock, 40.
Harbison (1992), 132–33.
Lalor, 137–39.

Access: The site is under the stewardship of the Office of Public Works. A key to the tower appears to be available locally from Mrs. Kelly at Autoview on Dublin Road, opposite the Gardaí Station (as described on the pillar west of the tower).

Map: OS 43

Parking: Limited; space for about 4 cars at the top of Church Road just south of the intersection with 187 (Main Street).

Amenities: Pub at corner of Station and Dublin Roads (R187 and 188).

Road past Lusk.

Route:
Lusk to Drogheda

Follow Main St. (R127) north into Skerries Rd. to the coast. The islands off Skerries are rich in lore of St. Patrick, with Church Island his legendary landing place. This coast was subject to repeated Viking raids, and while there were likely monasteries along the coast between Balbriggan and Drogheda, no remains have yet been uncovered. Continue to follow Skerries Road (R132) until it joins the N1, which follows the old Dublin Rd. into Drogheda. (Approximately 31.5 k/19.6 mi.)

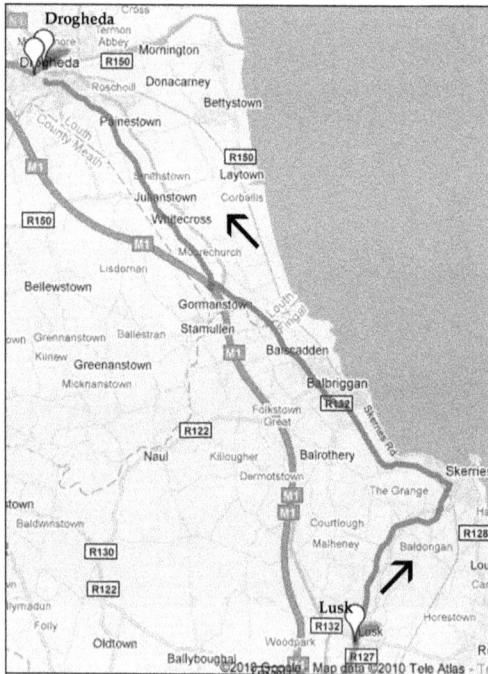

4. DROGHEDA

Map: OS 43

Amenities: Drogheda is a thriving town of shops, hotels and restaurants. Boyne Books at 56/57 West Street has a good local history selection and a café with a proprietor knowledgeable about the area and its history.

ST. MARY D'URSO

History: Known as the Old Abbey or the Hospital of St. Mary d'Urso, the Abbey of St. Mary d'Urso was founded c.1206 by Ursus de Swemele (Suamel) and his wife as a hospital for the poor and infirm. Legend holds that it occupies the site of a church that dates from the time of St. Patrick, who baptized the townspeople at a nearby well in 433. The *Annals of the Four Masters* records that it was raided and burned in 849 by Vikings. Excavations in 1989, however, revealed no remains earlier than the late twelfth century. It was an Augustinian house, and a house of the Crutched Friars by the end of thirteenth century; then reformed by the Observantine Friars in 1519. It was suppressed in 1556.

Remains: All that remains is a central belfry tower surmounting a Gothic archway, with another fragment supported on a similar arch to the east and a gable wall to the west.

Italica Picture Gallery:
http://gallery.me.com/egardiner#100328

65

Online references:
http://two.archiseek.com/2010/1206-abbey-of-st-mary-
    durso-drogheda-co-louth/
http://www.excavations.ie/Pages/Details
    .php?Year=&County=Louth&id=3481

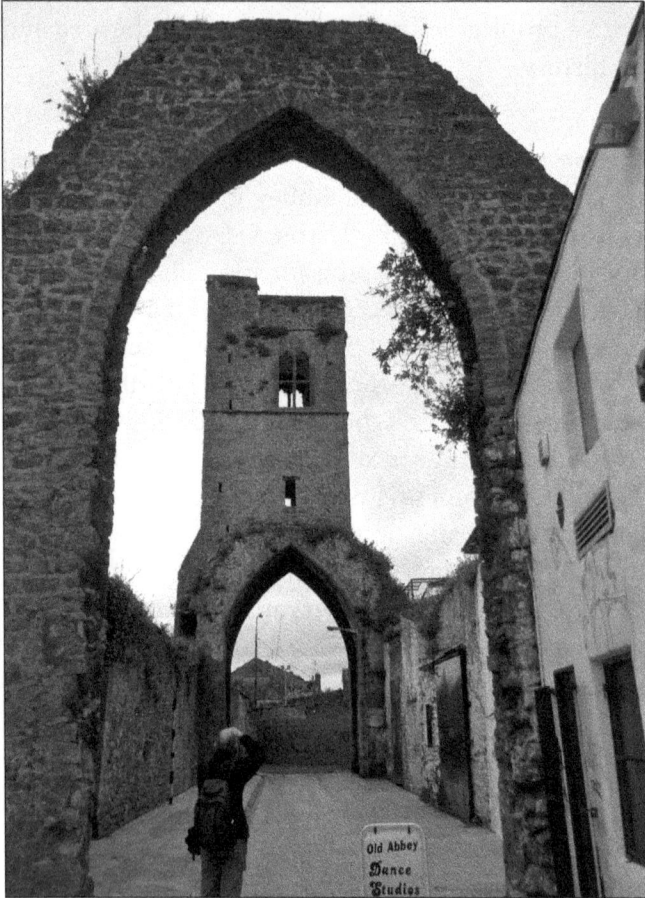

St. Mary d'Urso Abbey, Drogheda.

Bibliography:
Boylan, 188.
Casey & Rowan, 234.
Gwynn & Hadcock, 211.
Halpin, 452-510.

Access: The site is open as part of a public walkway connecting West Streets between Patrickswell Lane and Narrow West Street. There is no interior access to the tower.

Parking: A parking lot is on West Street.

St. Mary Magdalene

History: The Magdalene Tower of the fourteenth century was possibly a later addition to the once extensive Dominican friary founded here about 1224 by Lucas de Netterville, archbishop of Armagh. The abbey was surrendered in 1540, by which time the church was already in ruins.

Remains: The Magdalene Tower springs from a fine Gothic arch, above which there are two further stories connected by a spiral staircase. It is situated on the highest point north of the town.

Bibliography:
Boylan, 123–24.
Casey & Rowan, 236.
Gwynn & Hadcock, 224.
Harbison (1992), 234–35.

Online references:
http://two.archiseek.com/2010/1224-dominican-friary-drogheda-co-louth/

Access: There is no access to the tower, but as #4 on the Drogheda Heritage Trail, it is well cared for and clearly visible in a small park.

Magdalene Tower, Drogheda.

Route: Drogheda to Mellifont

The N51 leaves the west end of town via Trinity St. and reaches a traffic circle. This may have been the site of a stone and well dedicated to St. Patrick, which shows up on early nineteenth-century maps. At the circle take R168 as far as Begrath where a left-hand turn takes you onto Old Mellifont Rd. with the ruins of the abbey at its end. (Approximately 9 k/5.5 mi.)

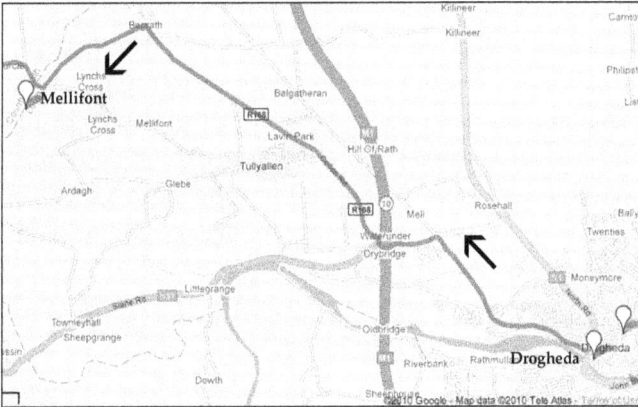

5. MELLIFONT

History: Mellifont (Fons Mellis = fountain of honey), sometimes called Drogheda, is Ireland's first Cistercian abbey, founded in 1142 by St. Malachy. It flourished until its closure in 1539. Ramon de Perellós (1397) mentions stopping here on the way to Lough Derg. Guillebert de Lannoy (1430) mentions stopping at Drogheda and may have been referring to Mellifont by this name.

Remains: There are extensive, although fragmentary, remains of Mellifont Abbey, including the gateway, the main outlines of the thirteenth-century church and domestic buildings. The finely carved octagonal lavabo with Romanesque arches, the main feature of the site, rises two stories, and there are the remains

Mellifont Abbey.

of a sixteenth-century chapel with belfry outside the abbey walls.

Italica Picture Gallery:
http://gallery.me.com/egardiner#100318

Online Resources:
http://www.heritageireland.ie/en/midlandseastcoast/
OldMellifontAbbey/

Bibliography:
Casey & Rowan, 387–93.
Boylan, 146–49.
Gwynn & Hadcock, 139.
Harbison (1992), 237–38.
Mellifont Abbey, The Old and the New.
The Story of Mellifont.

Access: The site, administered by the Office of Public Works, is generally open to the public. There is also a Visitor Centre open only during the summer months.

Map: OS 43

Parking: A parking lot is on site.

Amenities: The Visitor Centre is opened in the summer with a gift shop and toilets. Picnic area, no cafe.

Route: Mellifont to Slane

When you leave the abbey, make a left and continue on Old Mellifont Rd. until you reach the N2. A left turn will take you into Slane. A sharp right up Abbey View leads to the Hill of Slane. (Approximately 9 k/5.4 mi.)

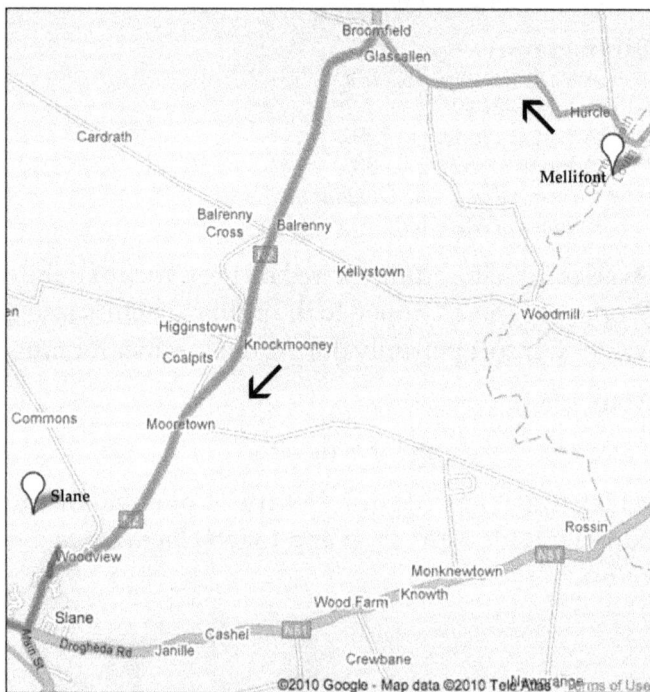

6. SLANE

History: What survives are the remains of a Franciscan friary of 1512 and a college, but the site is associated with St. Patrick, who is reputed to have built a fire

Hill of Slane.

73

here in 433 that could be seen from the Hill of Tara (visible in clear weather to the southwest).

This is also thought to be the site of the monastery of St. Erc (d. 513/4), founded shortly after the death of Patrick. The abbey was plundered in 833; the belfry burned in 950; the oratory fell down in 1028; it was generally plundered in 1156, 1161 and 1170, when it was probably no longer a monastery.

Remains: Ruins of a Franciscan friary and a Gothic tower (19 m, 62 ft high) atop the Hill of Slane (170 m, 560 ft). It may be possible to climb to the top of the tower. In the graveyard a tomb, apparently of great antiquity, known as St. Erc's Tomb, is recognizable from its two stones, which are shaped like gable ends.

Saints:
St. Erc. (Also Ercus, Erth, and Herygh.)

St. Erc is a fifth-century saint (d. 513/4), originally from Lilcach in Ireland, apparently active in Cornwall, but particularly associated with Slane. Legend tells that he was the one person to give homage to St.

Tomb Shrine of St. Erc.

Patrick when he confronted the Druids on the Hill of Slane in 433. He was later ordained and made bishop of Slane by Patrick. He also reportedly trained St. Brendan and established the school at Slane. A hermitage associated with him is on the north bank of the Boyne on the Slane Castle demesne. His feast day in November 2. There is a local tradition of relics.

The Cornish St. Erc, from the region near St. Ives, was brother to Sts. Uny and Ia. The town and church of St. Erth are named for him, and he is believed to be the same as the Irish saint. His feast day in Cornwall is October 31.

Relics: Two reliquaries, the staff shrine and bell shrine of St. Erc, are recorded in the *Annals of Ireland* (948) as being burned in the round tower.

The remains of the undated tomb, believed to be of great antiquity and known locally as St. Erc's Tomb or the Bishop's Tomb, apparently still formed part of the local funeral rites up until the twentieth century. The dead were reportedly carried three times around it and placed briefly on top of it before being buried.

Italica Picture Gallery:
http://gallery.me.com/egardiner#100272

Online references:
http://slanetourism.com/gpage1.html
http://www.slane.com/hillofslane.htm
http://sainterc.com/index.html
http://community.meath.ie/slanehistoricalsociety/index
  .php

Bibliography:
Boylan, 61–64.
Casey & Rowan, 471–74.
Gwynn & Hadcock, 44, 267, 274, 359, 361.
Harbison (1992), 267–68.

Access: Site is under the stewardship of the Office of Public Works and access to the site is open.

Parking: Ample parking outside the fence at the top of Abbey View road.

Nearby Interest Points: The Hermitage of St. Erc was presumably an oratory that contained relics of the saint. The date of the building itself — late fifteenth century — is too late to have actually been his dwelling, but almost certainly replaced earlier wooden structures. It is found within the Slane Castle demesne between the bank of the Boyne and St. Patrick's Church of Ireland. It is currently in a dilapidated condition and not open to public access.

St. Patrick's Catholic Church contains a fragment of a high cross found at Fennor on the south bank. It shows the Crucifixion on one face.

Map: OS 43

Amenities: Slane is a lovely village noted for the four Georgian mansions marking its crossroads, its castle and the stone bridge over the Boyne. It has a nice array of shops, restaurants and accommodations.

Route: *Slane to Donaghmore*

Returning down Abbey View, go right at the bottom into Chapel St. (N2), and right again at Main St. (N51). Here you are close to the ruins of the Hermitage of St. Erc, but they are not accessible. Follow the N51 southwest along the Boyne Valley. If you are traveling by foot, you should be able to travel the tow path along the river in various places, and at least from Oldbridge, the site of the Battle of the Boyne, just outside Drogheda, to Carrickdexter Weir, just past Slane, a total distance of more than 18 k (11 mi). The Inland Waterways Association is apparently working to return this same stretch of the river to navigable status. As you begin to descend into Navan along N51, the round tower of Donaghmore will be on the right. (Approximately 10 k/6.5 mi.)

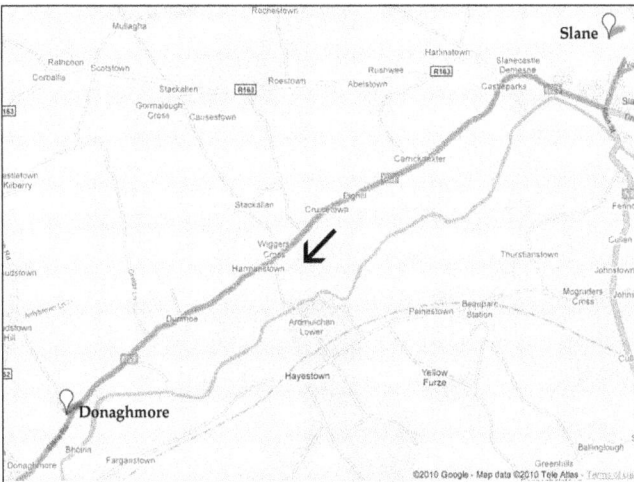

7. DONAGHMORE

History: Domhnach Mór (the big church) is believed to be the site of a monastery founded by St. Patrick, then passed on to St. Cassán, whose relics were

Round Tower, Donaghmore.

venerated here. Plundered 854, the church became parochial after the Anglo-Norman invasion (1171).

Remains: The round tower of the eleventh or twelfth century was restored in 1841 with the result that the stone at the top of the roof and the four windows at the top of the tower are missing, replaced about halfway up the shaft by windows, which face toward the four compass points. The doorway, although probably twelfth century, may not be original. It has unusual sculptural details: a crucified figure on the keystone and heads on the left and right jambs.

The nearby church was built in the sixteenth century, but it replaces a Romanesque church from which a head is incorporated into the south wall of the bell-tower of the church.

A fragment from a high cross now in the National Museum, Dublin, is associated with this site, but apparently is not currently on view there.

Saints:
ST. CASSÁN. (Also Cassan, Cassain.)

This early saint, a priest associated with Donaghmore — where his relics were venerated — is included among the favorite disciples of Patrick in the *Acts of St. Patrick,* thus a fifth-century saint. His feast day is June 4.

Relics: Tradition maintains that the relics of St. Cassán were venerated here, but nothing further is certain about the relics themselves.

Italica Picture Gallery:
http://gallery.me.com/egardiner#100261

Online references:
http://www.libraryireland.com/articles/
    DonaghmoreIDJ/index.php
http://roundtowers.org/donaghmore/index.htm

Bibliography:
    Casey & Rowan, 224–25.
    Gwynn & Hadcock, 34.
    Harbison (1992), 257.
    Lalor, 197–201.

Access: The site is under the stewardship of the Office of Public Works and access to the site is open.

Parking: Ample parking on the left after you turn off the N51.

Map: OS 42

Amenities: Navan, just down the hill, is a town with full facilities.

Remains of Church and Round Tower, Donaghmore.

Route: Donaghmore to Kells

Make a right onto the N51 towards Navan. Navan had an early monastery, which probably was converted into an Augustinian house in the twelfth century, but there are no visible remains. From Navan you pick up the old Navan–Kells Rd. This is now the busy N3, and although it has a very wide shoulder, if you are traveling by foot or bicycle, you might choose to follow a lane north from Donaghmore, which would avoid bustling Navan. This new road that takes you into R162 and R163 to Kells. (Approximately 18 k/11 mi.)

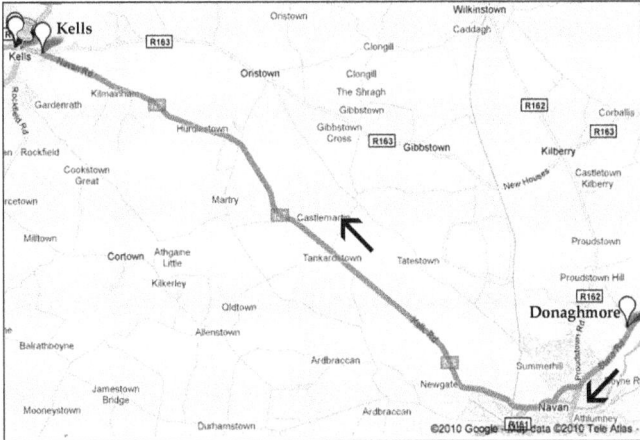

8. KELLS

History: Kells is mentioned as a stop in the itinerary of Guillebert de Lannoy (1430). Tradition holds that Kells (Ceanannas Mor) was the site of an early abbey founded c.550 by St. Columcille (Columba). In c.804 the monks of Iona, fleeing Viking raids, took refuge here and either joined or established an abbey on the grounds of St. Columba's Church. This abbey was made a cathedral in 1152, but after about 60 years the cathedral again became a parish church.

The Vikings plundered the abbey at Kells in 919, 950 and 969. It was raided by the Irish in the eleventh century and burned in 1111 and 1156. The town was burned in 1170 and 1315.

St. Mary's Abbey of the Augustinian Canons was founded 1140–48 under St. Malachy. Although its exact location is unknown, it was probably off Cannon Street/Oldcastle Road (R163). It was dissolved on 11 November 1539.

Remains: Round tower, four high crosses (plus the base of a fifth), and St. Columcille's House — each described separately below.

Saints:
ST. COLUMCILLE. (Also Columba.)

Columcille is particularly associated with Kells where his "house," possibly once a tomb shrine containing a tomb-shaped reliquary, remains an important monument. He is one of the Twelve Apostles of Ireland and one of the three patron saints of Ireland. Born December 7, 521 in Donegal, he died June 9, 597 on Iona.

According to legend, he founded the monastery at Kells while still a young man. He is credited as well with founding the monasteries at both Drumlane and Swords. In 563 he exiled himself to northern Scotland where he spent the next 34 years, either at Iona or on mission throughout the area.

In 804 when raiding parties attacked Iona, his followers moved to Kells, removing precious objects — probably including his relics — with them. Although there is some indication that his relics may have been removed to Downpatrick — where the remains of Patrick and Brigid, the other two patron saints of Ireland are revered — there is no clear evidence for this. Certain relics associated with Columcille were recorded at Kells, and one of the Station Island penitential beds is dedicated to him.

Relics: The shrine of the Great Gospels of Columcille (the famous Book of Kells) was produced c.800, close to the time when the monks of Iona fled their

monastery and resettled at Kells c.804. In 1006/7 the book was stolen from the sacristy of the Great Stone Church at Kells, but the manuscript was found under a sod two months later, without its priceless cover, and is now in Trinity College Library, Dublin.

There has been considerable scholarly exchange on whether the book was actually produced at Iona or Kells or partially at both. Some current research has tied it closely with other work produced at Kells that would seem to indicate a Kells origin, but Trinity College Library states that at present "there is no way of knowing."

The Staff Shrine or Crosier of Cuduilig (erenach of Kells, d. 1047) and Maelfinenn is now in the British Museum.

Italica Picture Gallery:
http://gallery.me.com/egardiner#100295

Online Resources:
http://www.kells-on-line.com/index.htm

Bibliography:
> Casey & Rowan, 327–33.
> Battersby (2000).
> Boylan, 45–49.
> Gwynn & Hadcock, 82, 181, 213, 318, 340, 351, 360.
> Harbison (1992), 261–63.

Parking: Ample street parking, but consider starting at the Kells Heritage Centre and walking with the Kells Heritage Trail Map:
http://www.kells-on-line.com/heritage_
> trail.htm

Map: OS 42

Amenities: Many places to eat throughout the town; accommodations also available.

Nearby Points of Interest:
The Kells Heritage Centre includes a book and gift shop and cafe and its collection incorporates a full-scale replica of the Market Cross, a multimedia

introduction to Kells, a model reconstruction of monastic Kells and material on the Book of Kells, including a facsimile, and various other artefacts of the crafts and culture of monastic Ireland. Unfortunately the centre is temporarily closed. Tourist information is available at Kells Town Hall, Headfort Place.

KELLS MARKET CROSS

History: This cross probably dates from about the middle of the ninth century and was moved from the monastery to the town crossroads in 1688 by Robert Balf and was restored and moved to its present location outside the Courthouse/Kells Heritage Centre four years after the base was struck by a bus in 1997. At the same time a replica was made, which is housed in the museum of the Heritage Centre. Originally this cross would probably have stood at one of the gates of the monastic city. Stories abound — it was used as a gallows, Dean Swift "lifted" the cross — and it shows clearly the ravages of an 1100-year history.

Remains: This high cross is quite deteriorated, probably as a result of its long tenure outside the walls of the church precinct. It originally stood to a height of c.4 m (12–13 ft). It is severely damaged at the top, worn away by acid rain, and the cap is missing. Decoration is almost completely representational, depicting primarily biblical subjects. (Detailed photos and descriptions are included in the picture gallery.)

Italica Picture Gallery:
http://gallery.me.com/egardiner#100311

Online References:
http://highcrosses.org/kells/index.htm

Market Cross, Kells.

http://www.megalithicireland.com/High%20Cross%20
Kells.htm

Bibliography:
Casey & Rowan, 332–33.
Boylan, 45–49.
Harbison (1992), 263.
Roe, 26–43.

KELLS ROUND TOWER

History: This round tower was built in the tenth century as part of the early monastery on the site. Like other towers, it may have been used as a look-out, belfry or refuge, where people and precious goods were hidden during raids.

Remains: Located on Cannon Street, where the wall surrounding St. Columba's Church grounds intersects the tower itself. The doorway is in the churchyard about 2 m (7 ft) from the ground. Instead of the usual four windows at the top, facing toward the four compass points, this tower has five, oriented toward the five town gates (Cannon, Carrick, Maudlin, Dublin and Farrell). Now without a cap, the tower reaches a height of 27 m (90 ft) from the original street level. There are six floors, but no staircase; access was by internal ladders. Each floor has one window. Some of the doorway's stonework is new, but the pattern of stonework indicates that there was some sculptural detail at the keystone and on the jambs. The door faces north and would have been in line with the south door of the great stone church.

Italica Picture Gallery:
http://gallery.me.com/egardiner#100285

Online References:
http://roundtowers.org/kells/index.htm
http://www.megalithicireland.com/High%20Cross%20
 Kells.htm

Round Tower, Kells.

Bibliography:
Casey & Rowan, 329.
Harbison (1992), 262.
Lalor, 201–3.
Roe, 62–63.

Access: The round tower is part of the Meath Heritage Trail with access to the grounds, although the tower itself is closed.

KELLS HIGH CROSSES

History: These crosses were probably produced in Kells and stood on the grounds of the great church where they may have been used either for instruction or for devotional meditation. (Detailed photos and descriptions are included in the picture gallery.)

Remains: The walled yard of St. Columba's Church contains four of the crosses found at Kells. The fifth, the Market Cross (pp. 85–86, above), is in front of the Kells Heritage Centre. Each cross here is named for its position in the churchyard.

The highly ornate South Cross, also known as the Cross of St. Patrick and St. Columba or the Cross of Kells, is the earliest and dates from at least as early as the second half of the eighth century. It is missing only its cap and is the least damaged of all the crosses in Kells. Decoration includes scriptural illustrations and abstract motifs.

South Cross, Kells.

The West Cross, or Ruined Cross, dates from about the middle of the ninth century. It is missing its head and part of its shaft, and the decoration that remains includes figurative motifs on the wide faces and abstract patterns on the narrow faces.

West, or Ruined, Cross, Kells.

The unfinished East Cross dates possibly from the twelfth century and, although scarcely decorated, is important for showing the preliminary preparation for the planned decoration.

Of the North Cross, the most recent of the crosses in Kells, only the base survives.

Italica Picture Gallery:
http://gallery.me.com/egardiner#100303

East Cross, Kells.

Online References:
http://www.megalithicireland.com/High%20Cross%20
    Kells.htm
http://www.kells-on-line.com/monsb.htm

Bibliography:
    Casey & Rowan, 329–33.
    Roe, 1966.

St. Columcille's (Columba's) House

History: This house, probably built to house the relics of St. Columcille, dates from the early ninth century and is characteristic of an oratory from the period. It once housed a 2-m (6-ft) bullaum stone, 0.3 m (1 ft) thick, called St. Columcille's Bed. This relic was stolen in the twentieth century.

Remains: St. Columcille's House is a one-story, barrel vaulted, rectangular building with a steep stone roof, probably of a later date. The orientation is east–west and there is a window over the eastern altar and a doorway, now blocked, at about 2 m (6–7 ft) above the present floor level, at the west end. The current entry leads to what would have been the basement; the wooden floor of the main chamber is no longer in place. There is a croft of three small chambers in the roof space with light provided by a small narrow opening. Legend, as well as the *Annals of the Four Masters* and the *Down Survey* of the seventeenth century, maintains the existence of an underground passage that led to St. Columba's Church.

Relics: A tomb-shaped Shrine of Columcille may have been venerated in St. Columcille's House. Now lost, it was mentioned twice in the *Annals of Ireland* (875, 1127), but was not particularly identified as belonging to this site. St. Columcille's Bed (a stone

St. Columcille's House, Kells.

slab), now lost, was in the house until probably the 1930s.

The *Annals of Ireland* (1034) also mentions a bed of Columcille but notes that it was lost at sea. Bullaun stones are sometimes referred to as beds and this term can also refer to the rudderless stone boats on which saints legendarily sailed. Although ancient ballaun stones have a characteristic hemispherical indent, the name is widely applied to large stones with any indentation. Often they are associated with a saint and hold water that is considered holy. On the Connemarra coast there is such a bullaum identified with Columcille. In Spain is another famous stone that reportedly carried the body of St James from the Holy Land to Galicia — and on which he was first buried at Iria Flavia, near Santiago de Compostela.

Online References:
http://homepage.eircom.net/~kellsnet/monsc.htm
http://www.megalithicireland.com/High%20Cross%20
  Kells.htm

Bibliography:
  Boylan, 45–49.
  Casey & Rowan, 328–29.
  Harbison (1992), 263.
  Roe, 60–62.

Access: The house is part of the Meath Heritage Trail; and while generally locked, a note at the gate indicates where the key can be located.

Parking: There is ample street parking, but consider walking through this delightful town from the Kells Heritage Centre with the Kells Heritage Trail Map: http://www.kells-on-line.com/heritage_trail.htm

Route: Kells to Castlekeeran

From the round tower at the top of Kells, Cannon St. leads west into Oldcastle Rd. (R163). Past Commons of Lloyd, at Sheeny, a small road on the right goes N and NW through Castlepole to Castlekeeran, where at 3 k (1.9

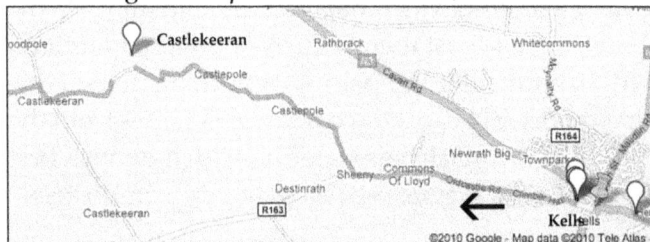

mi) a sign marked SN107 on the south side of the road, behind a tree, points through a farmyard to the remains of the abbey. Farther along this road is the clearly visible well. (Approximately 5.8 k/3.6 mi.)

9. CASTLEKEERAN

Italica Picture Gallery:
http://gallery.me.com/egardiner#100243

Parking: Along the side of the road.

Map: OS 42

Amenities: Kells (5.8 k/3.6 mi E) is a town with a full array of facilities.

ST. CIARÁN'S MONASTERY & HIGH CROSSES

History: The monastery was founded St. Ciarán (d. 770/78), plundered by Norseman in 949 and burnt in 1170.

Remains: Around the ruins of the church (in the graveyard hidden behind a copse) there are three high crosses with some decoration, but no figural sculpture. There is also the base of a fourth cross, an early-Christian, two-armed cross-slab and an Ogham stone.

Saints:
ST. CIARÁN. (Also Kieran.)
    There are many St. Ciaráns, some of them famous, but little is known about the founder of this abbey at Castlekeeran, who is called St. Kieran of Disert-Kieran, and referred to by the Irish annalists as "Kieran the Devout" or "Kieran the Pious." He is thought to be the author of a "Life of St. Patrick." Although some place his death anywhere between 770 and 778, he is reported to have died in 775 on

June 14. His feast day is celebrated on that day, but a pattern day takes place at the well at Castlekeeran on the first Sunday of August.

Bibliography:
Casey & Rowan, 221–22.
Gwynn & Hadcock, 375.
Harbison (1992), 256.

St. Ciarán's Monastery & High Cross, Castlekeeran.

Access: The site is open, but you must pass through a private farmyard. Past the sheds on the left there is a stile into the enclosed abbey grounds.

St. Ciarán's Well

Remains: A well and (modern) oratory. A nearby tree is hung with votive offerings. The annual pattern day occurs on the first Sunday of August.

St. Ciarán's Well, Castlekeeran.

Online References:
http://homepage.eircom.net/%257Ekellsnet/ciaran.htm
http://www.askaboutireland.ie/reading-room/history-
    heritage/folklore-of-ireland/the-holy-wells-of-
    meath-f/keenahene-loughan/

Bibliography:
Harbison (1992), 256.

Access: This tranquil site, about 0.2 mi past St. Ciarán's Monastery, is open. The well and oratory are clearly visible to the north of the road.

Route: Castlekeeran to Kilmore

This is the longest stretch of the Pilgrim's Way without a station. At almost 50 k (over 30 mi), there probably would have been at least one place for a pilgrim on foot to stop. Maps of monastic Ireland identify five possible places in this region (all hospitals or hospices: Munterconnaught, Clonkeiffy, Ballymachugh, Crosserlough and Denn),

Kilmore.

although little documentary evidence and no physical remains have been identified.

We know that a Dublin Rd. to Sligo passed through Kells, Oldcastle, Roebuck, Mt. Pallas, Ballintemple, Bellanangh to Crossdony near Kilmore. The modern road leads west from Castlekeeran, then south to R163, which leads into R154 through Oldcastle, into R194, and follows this Dublin Rd., which changes into R199 just before Crossdony. Here, just southwest of Cavan, a right into R198 leads to the bottom of the hill that is topped by the church of Kilmore. (Approximately 49 k/30.5 mi.)

10. KILMORE

History: At Kilmore (Cill More = great church), Cavan Co., legend maintains that a monastery was founded by St. Felim or Feidhlimidh in the sixth or seventh century. A larger church (the present parish house) was constructed c.1400. The new cathedral of St. Féithlimidh is nineteenth-century but incorporates a Romanesque doorframe and archivolt, which some sources say originated at Tonymore, from where it was moved to Holy Trinity Abbey (founded 1237 or 1239) on Trinity Island (Dair-Inis = Island of Oaks), in Lough Oughter. When Holy Trinity was dissolved in 1551, the doorway was moved first to Slandore then to the old cathedral at Kilmore, where it served as the main entrance. Finally, upon the construction of

Romanesque Archivolt and
Door Jamb Decoration, Kilmore.

the new cathedral, it was incorporated there as the vestry door (1860).

Remains: The vestry door on the north side of the new cathedral (1860) has a carved Hiberno-Romanesque doorway with beaded hood-molding, decorated with animal, geometric and foliage motifs. The old cathedral from c.1400 is greatly altered, but still stands and now serves as a parish house. It was possibly built on the site of an earlier foundation that was reputedly established here. It became an episcopal seat in 1453/4. There is also a holy well (seventeenth or eighteenth century).

Saints:
St. Feidhlimidh. (Also Felim.)

St. Feidhlimidh was probably a hermit of the sixth or seventh century. The first known bishop of Kilmore, he is patron of the diocese. He died on August 9, which is designated as his feast day.

Relics: The Staff Shrine of Feidhlimidh is mentioned in the *Annals of Ireland* (840). It is now lost and was not conclusively identified with this site.

Italica Picture Gallery:
http://gallery.me.com/egardiner#100350

Online References:
http://www.breifnehistory.com/index.html
http://www.cornafean.com/kilmore.htm

Bibliography:
Gwynn & Hadcock, 87–89.
Harbison (1992), 54.
O'Donovan, 201.
Wood, 47, 49, 52–54.

Access: An avenue, on the left as you travel north on Route 198 from Ricehill to Tonymore, leads up to the cathedral, which is perched on a hill. The door, at the eastern end of the north side, is clearly visible and seems to be lighted at night.

Parking: There is parking in a lot past the cathedral and parish house.

Map: OS 34

Amenities: Nearby Cavan (5.6 k / 3.5 mi NE) is a town with a full array of facilities.

Route: Kilmore to Drumlane

With the road from Kilmore to Drumlane we enter the region of lakes, and from here many medieval and early-modern travelers may have proceeded by boat. The contemporary waterways and islands are not necessarily what they were

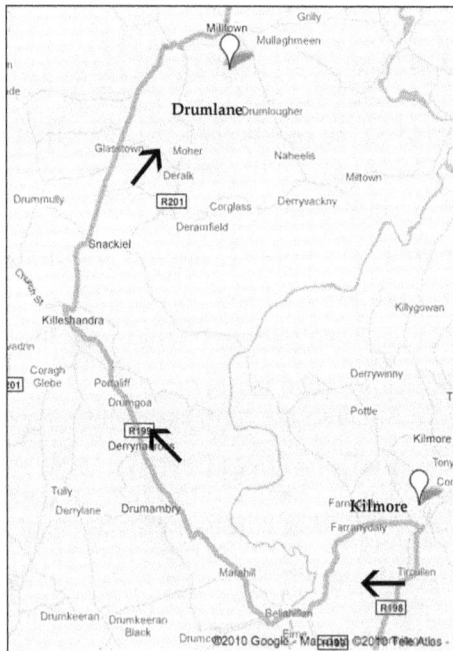

in the Middle Ages: bridges were added and canals were dug to make travel easier both by land and water. By car, a sharp right at the bottom of the Kilmore hill brings you back to R199 to Kileshandra, where a right into R201 leads directly to Milltown. At the middle of town a sharp right leads almost directly south on an unmarked road to Drumlane Abbey.

An alternate route, if you are traveling by foot or bike, takes the same road west from the bottom of the hill at Kilmore, but in less than a mile or about a kilometer, a turn to the right leads to and through Kilkeen Forest Park (one footbridge at Lough Oughter prevents through-traffic by car). This road eventually leads out to R201 toward Milltown. (Approximately 20 k/12 mi.)

Road to Drumlane.

11. DRUMLANE

History: Drumlane (Droim Leathan = broad ridge) Monastery was already flourishing in 550. It may have been founded by St. Columcille and restored by St. Maedhóg. In the mid-twelfth century (1143–48) — during the time of St. Malachy — as St. Mary's Priory, it became a monastery of the Augustinian Canons from St. Mary's Abbey, Kells. There was extensive fire

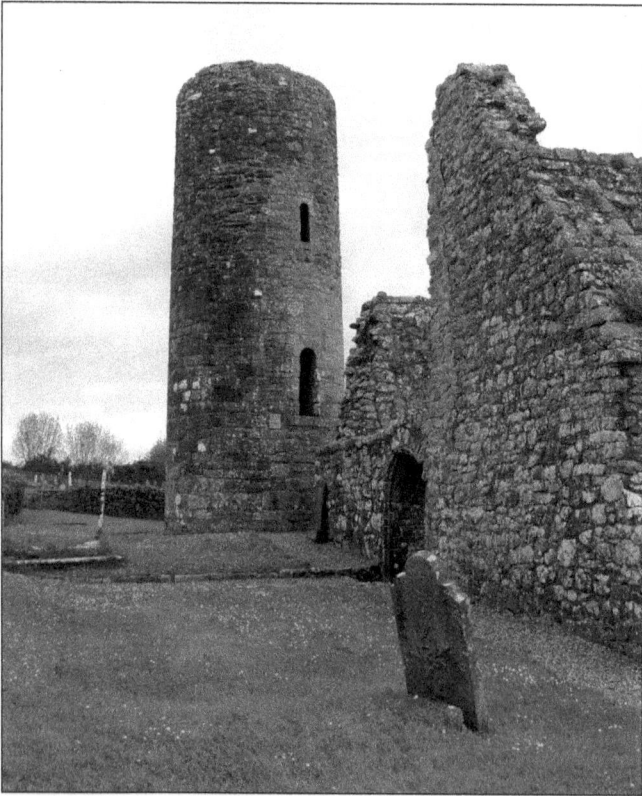

Drumlane Round Tower and Abbey.

damage in 1246, and in 1431 there was an appeal for aid in building a cloister and refectory. The monastery was dissolved in 1570/1.

Remains: There is a round tower, with the lower part dating from the tenth or eleventh century and the upper part dating possibly from the fifteenth century. The tower has a round-headed door and windows. On the north face are much weathered carvings, said to be of a cock and hen. There are also the remains of a church dating possibly from the late thirteenth century, but with alterations probably from the fifteenth century, and some later parts (seventeenth century) at the west end. On the exterior of the east window there are sculpted heads (two kings and a bishop), as well as sculpted heads on the west doorway.

Saints:

St. Columcille (pp. 82–83, above).

St. Maedhóg. (Also Maedoc, Mogue, Aedan, Aodán, Aidan.)

Maedhóg is a late fifth-/early sixth-century saint from the Cavan area, born either on Inis Brechmaighe, or St. Mogue's Island, in Templephort Lough, or on an island in nearby Brackley Lough, c.555/58/60 to Sedna, a chieftain of Connaught, and his wife Eithne. Along the Pilgrim's Way, he is particularly associated with Drumlane. He founded Drumlane and two other monasteries: Rossinver (Ros Inbhir) in Leitrim and Ferns in Wexford, where he was elected its first bishop about 598.

He was educated in Wales by St. David and had a long friendship with St. Molaise of Devenish. Many miracles and legends are associated with his life, including the resurrection of three children drowned in Lough Erne and the creation of the Gillaroo trout, which formed from the leftovers, thrown into Lough Melvin, of a chicken served on a Friday that he had turned into a trout so he could eat it. He was noted for his benevolence and hospitality. He died in 625/6 or 632 and was buried at Ferns. His feast day is January 31.

Relics: Two important reliquaries are connected to this site. The tomb-shaped Breac Maedhóg from the eleventh/twelfth century, with its leather satchel, is now in the National Museum of Ireland, Dublin. St.

Breac Maedhóg.
Reproduced with the kind permission of the National Museum of Ireland.

Molaise, after returning from a pilgrimage to Rome, reportedly gave Maedhóg a number of relics for the Breac Maedhóg, including Hair of the Virgin Mary and St. Martin's Ankle Bone.

The Bell-Shrine of St. Maedhóg is now in the Armagh Public Library, where it is on display in a glass case, along with a remnant of the actual bell, the Clog Mogue.

Italica Picture Gallery:
http://gallery.me.com/
egardiner#100334

Bell Shrine of St. Maedhóg.
Published with the kind permission of the Armagh Public Library ©.
Photograph by Paul Eliasberg.

Online References:
http://www.drumlane.ie/index.php?page=monestry
http://drumlaneparish.net/abbey.html

Bibliography:
Gwynn & Hadcock, 170.
Harbison (1992), 53–54.
Lalor, 107–9.
O'Donovan, 197–98.
Wood, 61, 72–73, 75.

Access: This site is under the care of the Office of Public Works. The site is open to visitors.

Parking: There is parking to the right of the road above the church.

Map: OS 27

Amenities: Milltown has some limited options. Butlersbridge (9.6 k/6.6 mi) has a pub/restaurant and Belturbet (7.0 k/4.3 mi) has several.

Route: Drumlane to Aghalurcher

From Milltown on the R201, head north until the road forks at N87, taking a right, and then at the circle a left into the N3. Follow the Belturbet Road, which will become the A609. At Derrylin a right on the B127 leads across Trasna Island to the east side of Upper Lough Erne and up toward Aghalurcher. A sign on the right, just before Rossgad, indicates the church. (Approximately 27 k/17 mi.)

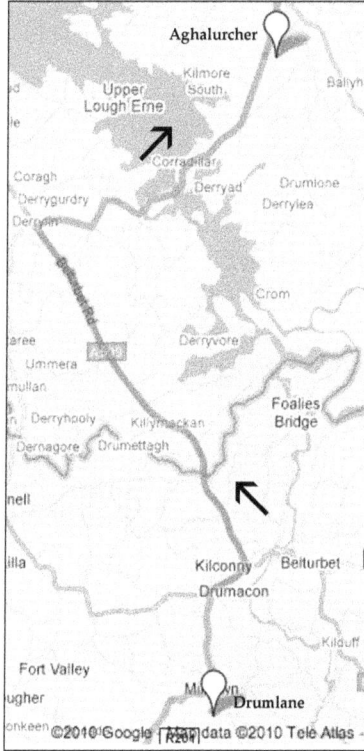

12. AGHALURCHER

History: Aghalurcher Monastery was established in the late sixth/early seventh century by St. Ronan and dedicated to him in the ninth century. The site is also associated with St. Feidhlimidh (of Kilmore). Excavations uncovered the foundations of a massive battered (i.e., inward leaning) east wall, probably dating from a remodeling, which is recorded for 1447 when a new roof was installed. Apparently a murder on the altar in 1484, which constituted a sacrilegious act, may have led to the subsequent abandonment of the church. (Aghalurcher = the field of the cast, reflecting the legend that the site was chosen by the throw of a javelin or sling stone.)

Aghalurcher.

Remains: There is the ruin of a medieval church on the site of a pre-Norman monastery. A small vault north of the church (locked) is probably late, but contains a single twelfth-century gravestone with Romanesque decoration, as well as loose carved stones from the church. The gateway to the churchyard also incorporates massive stones reused from the church, including a carved head over the arch.

At the Fermanagh County Museum (the Castle, Enniskillen) two twelfth-century sculptures from this site show a male exhibitionist figure and a figure bearing a staff and a book (in a shrine or leather sachel). The latter figure may have been part of a shrine of St. Ronan.

113

Saints:
ST. RONAN.

There are at least twelve Irish St. Ronans. The one associated with the Pilgrim's Way to Lough Derg is a late sixth-/early seventh-century saint connected to Aghalurcher. Legend claims he was the son of Aedh Dubh of the royal family of Airgialla. He is listed in the *Martyrology of Donegal* as Ronan, son of Aedh of Achadh-Fharcha. His feast day is recorded as December 23.

Italica Picture Gallery:
http://gallery.me.com/egardiner#100332

Online References:
http://irishantiquities.bravehost.com/fermanagh/
aghalurcher/aghalurcher.html

Bibliography:
Gwynn & Hadcock, 372.
Harbison (1992), 137.
Rowan, 361.
Wood, 47–48, 50, 56–58, 62, 91, 95–96.

Access: The site is maintained by the Department of the Environment for Northern Ireland and is open to visitors.

Parking: The driveway has limited parking.

Map: OS 27

Amenities: Lisnaskea (3 k/2 mi N) is a market town with a full array of services.

Route: Aghalurcher to Devenish

This was almost certainly a journey made by boat from Upper Lough Erne past Enniskillen, but now it's normally a journey along the B127 through Lisnaskea (with its distinguished market cross). From there the A34 probably follows the old Dublin Rd. that once led to Ballyshannon along the west shore of Lower Lough Erne. At the A4, a left will bring you to Enniskillen. There were important monasteries in this area but remains, if they exist at all, are inaccessible: Galloon, Cleenish, Derrybrusk, Derryvullen, Inishkeen, Lisgoole and Rossorry. At Enniskillen you pick up the A32 heading NE, and follow it until the turnoff on the left for the Trory Point Ferry Station, where a boat will take you to Devenish with its round tower, high cross, and other remains. (Approximately 27 k/17 mi.)

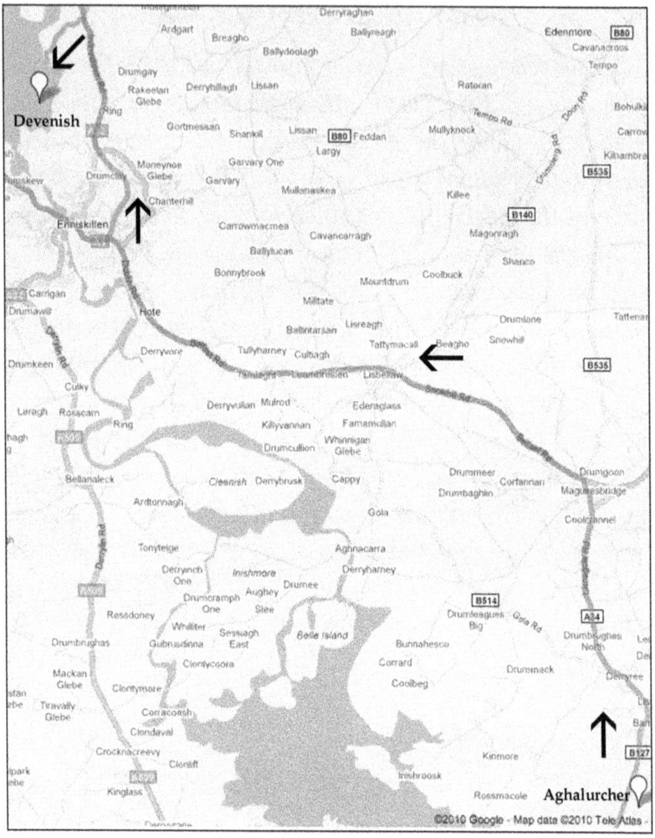
Devenish
Aghalurcher
©2010 Google - Map data ©2010 Tele Atlas

13. DEVENISH

History: The Devenish (= Isle of the Oxen) Monastery was founded in the sixth century by St. Molaise (Laisrén) who died in 564. The Abbey Church of Saint Mary, founded 1130, became an Augustinian establishment. It existed side-by-side with the older priory. Burned in 1157 and 1360, the site was deserted by 1607.

Remains: There are extensive remains, including a twelfth-century round tower with a sculpted and decorated cornice, next to the foundation of another, probably earlier round tower; the thirteenth-century Great Church (Teampull Mór) with the bullaun stone that, legend holds, carried St. Molaise across the sea; St. Molaise's House (1157), which was probably a

Devenish.

117

tomb shrine; the Priory of St. Mary, now mostly the remains of the monastery rebuilt in 1449; and a late medieval high cross.

Saints:

ST. MOLAISE. (Also Laisrén.)

St. Molaise of Devenish (d. 564) was the subject of two lives, one Irish and one Latin, both full of historical and legendary details. He is one of the Twelve Apostles of Ireland. He is reported to have studied under St. Finián of Clonard (d. 549) and to have been a friend of St. Maedhóg of Drumlane. Molaise made a pilgrimage to Rome and returned with relics, some of which he shared with Maedhóg, while others — of Peter and Paul, Lawrence and Clement — were buried with him on Devenish, helping to make it an important pilgrimage spot. Some of his own relics — his house or tomb shrine and his bullaun stone or bed — remain on Devenish. His feast day is September 12.

Relics: In addition to the tomb shrine of St. Molaise and his bullaun stone, which are on Devenish, other relics include the Soiscél Molaise — also known as the Shrine of the Gospel Book of Molaise

Soiscél Molaise.
Reproduced with the kind permission of the National Museum of Ireland.

Lough Erne Shrines.
Reproduced with the kind permission of the National Museum of Ireland.

— an early eleventh-century book–shrine (the manuscript is missing); and two late eighth- or early ninth-century tomb-shaped reliquaries, known as the Lough Erne shrines, which were found in Lough Erne, one inside the other, in 1891 and presumed to be from Devenish. These reliquaries are now in the collection of the National Museum of Ireland, Dublin. The Latin and Irish lives of Molaise also mention a bell, which is unidentified.

Italica Picture Gallery:
http://gallery.me.com/egardiner#100374

Online references:
http://www.ni-environment.gov.uk/devenish.htm
http://roundtowers.org/devenish/index.html
http://www.discoverireland.com/za/ireland-things-to-see-and-do/listings/product/?fid=NITB_2899
http://www.cassidyclan.org/devinish.htm

Bibliography:
Gwynn & Hadcock, 33, 153, 169, 362.
Harbison (1992), 15, 19, 138–39, 142.
Lalor, 142–45.
Rowan, 232-25.
Wood, 47, 51–52, 61, 63–70, 91–92, 95–96.

Access: The site, open to visitors for set hours and seasons, is in lower Lough Erne and is maintained by the Northern Ireland Environment Agency, which runs a ferry service from Easter through September from Trory Point on the eastern shore of the lake (5 k/3 mi N of Enniskillen). There is limited space on the ferry. Access is also possible as part of a tour of Lower Lough Erne on the MV Kestrel from Enniskillen.

Parking: There is limited parking at the Trory Point dock.

Map: OS 17

Amenities: On the island are an interpretative centre and toilets; Enniskillen (5 k/3 mi S) is a large town with a full array of services.

Route: Devenish to Inishmacsaint

While an easy boat ride would have taken the pilgrim north to Inishmacsaint, if you are traveling by car you will need to backtrack to Enniskillen, and following the signs for Belleek and the A46, take Lough Shore Drive. A turnoff on the right at Ross Point leads to a parking area, from which you can walk out, across a pontoon barge, to the island. (Approximately 19.5 k/12 mi.)

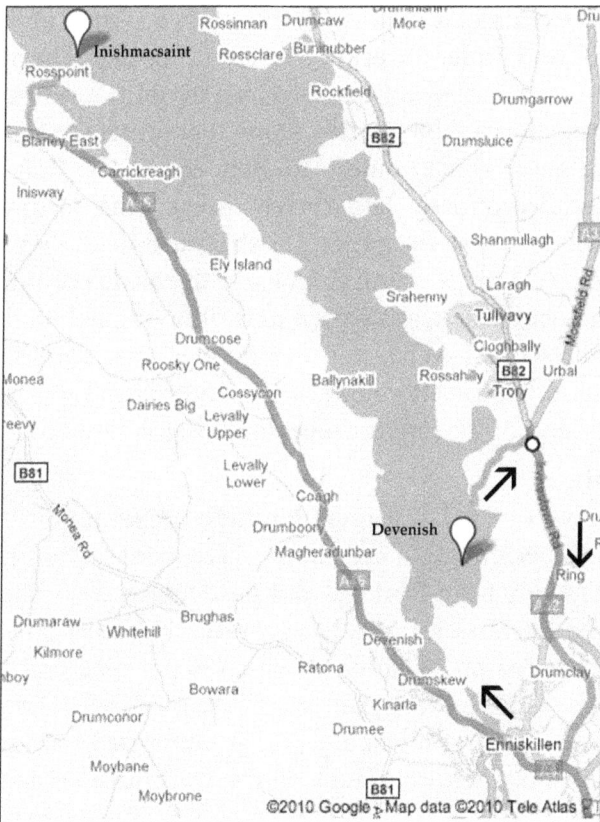

14. INISHMACSAINT

History: Inishmacsaint (Inis-maige-samh = Island of the Sorrel Plain) was founded by St. Nennid (d. 523/30). An abbot, Fiannamail, is recorded in 718. The monastery was probably damaged during the raids of the ninth and tenth centuries.

Remains: An early stone cross and the remains of a church are found here. The cross, which is just SW of the church, is plain with rectangular panels at the ends and under the arms. The top is missing. The tall thin cross is currently formed by a stone, mounted on a base, topped by another stone that forms the arms and head. It may date from between the tenth and twelfth centuries. The church shows work of three periods: a pre-Romanesque structure in the west, tenth/eleventh century; an early thirteenth-century expansion eastward with a new door opened on the south to replace the now-closed west door; and the late medieval alteration of the south window. The east end of the interior reveals two cupboard spaces.

Saints:
St. NENNID. (Also Ninnid, Ninnidh or Nenn.)

St. Nennid is an early sixth-century saint, originally from Donegal, but particularly associated with Inishmacsaint in Lough Erne. His feast day is celebrated on 18 January, which is the date that he died, but the exact year is unknown (523–30). Local places bearing his name, and so identified with his mission, include: Glenwinney (Ninnidh's Glen),

Ninnidh's Hill above Roscor, nearby Ninnidh's Well and Knockninny.

He was one of the Twelve Apostles of Ireland and a grandson of the High King Laoire. He was educated at Clonard under St. Finián. His contemporaries there

Inishmacsaint.

included St. Ciarán of Clonmacnoise, who visited Inishmacsaint in 534; and St. Molaise of Devenish and St. Maedhóg of Drumlane, who were close friends of Nennid. Legend maintains that he was one of the twelve students supported on the milk of St. Ciarán's Dun Cow. He made the island of Inishmacsaint his headquarters around 523.

Relics: St. Nennid's Bell was in the Castle Caldwell Collection until 1877, when it was sold at auction to Robert Day of Cork (who sketched the drawing). When Day's collection was sold in 1913, this bell was not part of the sale. Although for some time it was identified with a bell in the National Museum of Edinburgh (probably St.

St. Nennid's Bell.

Ninian's Bell, formerly from the collection of John Bell), the location of St. Nennid's Bell is presently unknown. (See Ó Floinn, 2006.)

Italica Picture Gallery:
http://gallery.me.com/egardiner#100214

Online References:
http://www.shee-eire.com/Sites&Monuments/Celtic-Cross/Fermanagh/Inishmacsaint/imstccinfo.htm
http://www.ni-environment.gov.uk/whiteisland.pdf

Bibliography:
Gwynn & Hadcock, 38.
Parke (1982).
Rowan, 318–19.

Access: There are signs at the lot pointing toward a lane that brings you to a pontoon that crosses to the island. The remains are visible above at the top of the hill, slightly to the right of the pontoon. The site, although in the middle of cow pasture, is accessible and administered by the Northern Ireland Environment Agency.

Parking: There is ample parking in the lot at the end of the road.

Map: OS 17

Amenities: Enniskillen (14.2 k/8.8 mi S) is a large town with a full array of services.

Route: Inishmacsaint to White Island

Again, travel by boat would have taken, and still can take, the pilgrim directly to White Island. If your are traveling by land, however, it is necessary to backtrack again through Enniskillen, this time taking the A32 just past Trory Point where the B82 veers to the left and brings you to Castle Archdale Country Park, where the signs will lead to the marina on the lakeshore. Here a ferry operates to White Island with its church remains and famous sculptural figures. (Approximately 32 k/20 mi.)

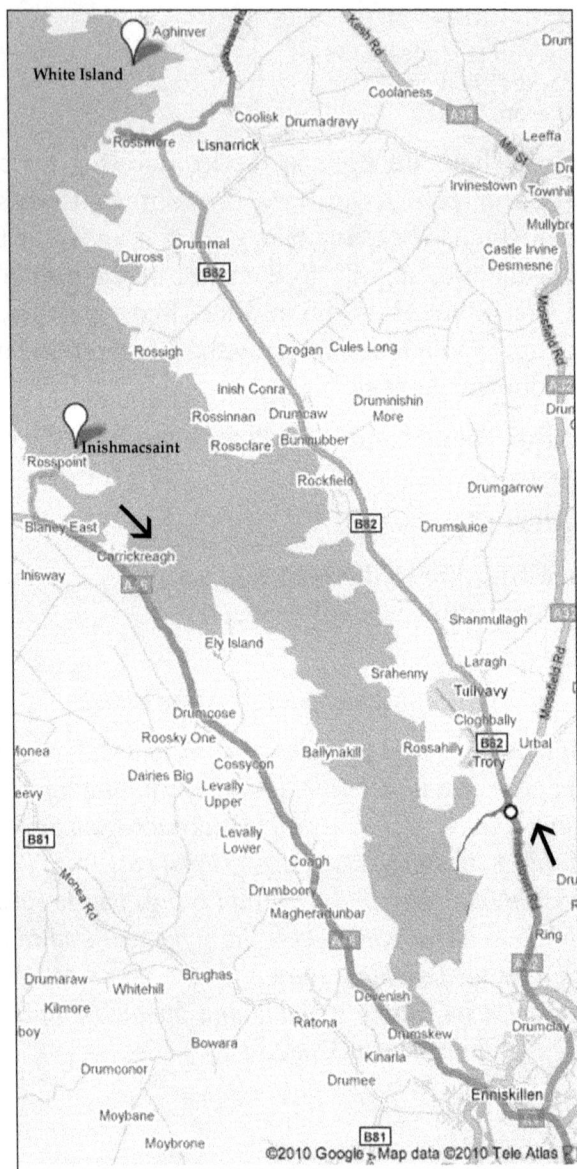

15. WHITE ISLAND

History: The early name for the island is unknown and the site is no longer associated with any saint, but White Island was clearly the site of an early church,

Romanesque Doorway, with view of figures, White Island.

probably a monastery. Excavations in 1959 showed that the church site was previously occupied by a wooden structure.

Remains: There is a ruined church of c.1200 with a fine and complete round-headed Romanesque doorway — the only complete one in Northern Ireland. A bank and ditch surround the site of the church and probably indicated a monastic boundary, which would have enclosed the usual monastic buildings, including a guest house, all built of wood.

The site is famous for the six (2 small and 4 large) archaic stone figures, which are set into the north wall of the current structure. Another unfinished sculpture from the group indicates that they were carved on site. The figures pre-date the church and were found as building materials incorporated into its wall. While it is difficult to identify the figures exactly, one proposal suggests that they represent pilgrims and another that they include symbolic representations of Christ. They include a cross-legged female; a figure with a book; a figure with a bell and crozier, a figure with a staff and pouch; a figure with two mythological beasts; a knight with a sword and shield.

It is possible to regard the first, fourth and sixth figures as pilgrims: the first — a Sheelanagig — was a representation of lust, and therefore a likely penitential pilgrim; the fourth has the typical pilgrim emblems: pouch and staff; and the last figure, a knight, like Knight Owein, was a familiar pilgrim who would be exiled to expiate sins committed in war. The second and third figures appear to represent saints holding their book, staff and bell reliquaries, which pilgrims would travel to see. The fifth figure remains unexplained in this system.

The alternate interpretation regards the second figure with the book as Christ the Missionary or Evangelist; the third as Christ the Shepherd; the fourth as King David, a prototype of Christ; the fifth as Christ the divine and the human; and the sixth as Christ in triumph on the Last Day. The first figure remains unexplained in this system.

Italica Picture Gallery:
http://gallery.me.com/egardiner#100361

Online References:
http://www.megalithicireland.com/index.html
http://www.fermanaghlakelands.com/P2900-White-Island-Lough-Erne-Kesh-Enniskillen.aspx
http://www.ni-environment.gov.uk/whiteisland.pdf

Bibliography:
Chambers, 2002.
Harbison (1992), 18, 141–42.
Rowan, 506–8.
Wood, 25–31, 35–42, 46, 50.

Access: There are at least two White Islands in Lough Erne. This one is off the east shore of the lake at Castle Archdale harbor. The passenger ferry to White Island runs daily in the summer and on weekends in late spring and early autumn. Otherwise, with your own boat, the site appears to be open and accessible at all times under the administration of the Northern Ireland Environment Agency.

Map: OS 17

Parking: Plenty of parking at Castle Archdale Country Park.

Amenities: Toilets and a tea shop at Castle Archdale Country Park.

Route: White Island to Lough Derg

Traveling by boat a pilgrim would continue to the north shore of Lough Erne, possibly stopping at Boa Island, before landing near Termon McGrath Castle, between the Termon and Waterfoot Rivers. From here it's a short distance to Pettigo. By land, the road leads back through Castle Archdale Country Park to the B82, where a left leads into the A35 to Pettigo. A right in the town square into Mill St. leads to St. Patrick's Terrace, through Tullycarn, Carn (Templecarne) and Tawlaght. A path from Templecarne, just west of today's road, probably led to the lake, but the modern road leads shortly to a turnoff on the left to the parking lot, Visitor Centre and ferry station for Station Island, as well as the start of the Medieval Irish Pilgrim Path. (Approximately 22.5 k/14 mi.)

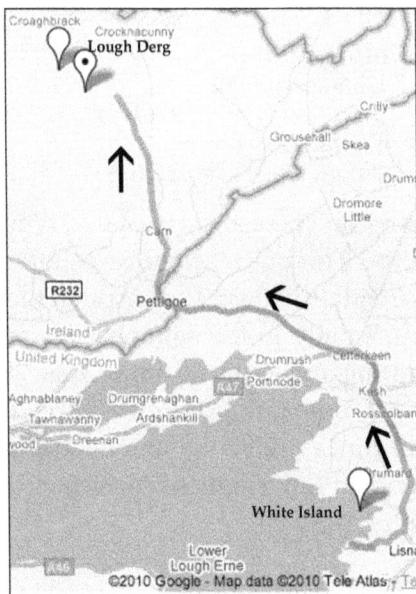

16. Lough Derg

Introduction

Arriving at the final destination of a long pilgrimage is momentous and memorable, but arriving at Lough Derg is very different from arriving at Rome, Santiago de Compostela, Jerusalem or even Canterbury. There is no extraneous activity here, no hubbub, simply the calm and quiet of a northern lake. The pilgrim is surrounded by nature: primarily by sky and water. Whether or not you take the boat to Station Island to participate in the ritual pilgrimage of the site itself, the experience of this place has its own rewards.

At the shore of Lough Derg, where the boats from Station Island dock, there is a large parking lot and a Visitors Centre with an exhibition space, rest rooms and an information desk. A small pavilion near the dock shelters pilgrims as they wait for the boats. A large statue of St. Patrick as a young pilgrim is nearby, and behind this statue is the beginning of the path that leads to Saints Island.

The Pilgrim Path along the lake (pp. 141–43, below) is the alternative for anyone who arrives at Lough Derg off-season (i.e., between August 16th and June 1) or is disinclined to undertake the rigors of fasting and prayer.

Location

Donegal's Lough Derg is a 9-square kilometer (2200-acre) lake about 21 k (13 mi) in circumference, 137 m (450 ft) above sea level. From the Ordnance

Survey Map 11 (1:50,000) there appear to be 29 islands, the principal ones being Station Island and Saints Island, which was probably once known as St. Dabheoc's Island. Others are named: Derg More, Derg Beg, Trough, Bull's, Gravelands, Kelly's,

Lough Derg.

Philipboy, Allingham's, Boat, Friar's, Goose Lodge and Inishgoosk. This region was originally known as Termon Dabheoc, after St. Dabheoc, and later Termon McGrath, after the family who were coarbs — hereditary stewards — here from 1290. The remains of their castle are near the northern shore of Lough Erne, south of Pettigo.

SAINTS

ST. BRENDAN. (Also Bréanainn.)

St. Brendan's association with the Pilgrim's Way to Lough Derg is tangential. He is, of course, Brendan the Navigator, one of the Twelve Apostles of Ireland, an early monastic saint, born c.484 on the coast of Kerry. One of the penitential beds on Station Island bears his name. He is also associated with St. Erc of Slane, who baptized him and later educated him and ordained him a priest in 512. Brendan died in 577 and is buried in Clonfert Cathedral. His feast day is May 16.

ST. BRIGID. (Also Brigit, Bridget, Bridgit, Bríd or Bride, Naomh Bríd.)

St. Brigid of Kildare's association with the Pilgrim's Way to Lough Derg is nebulous. She is one of Ireland's patron saints along with Saints Patrick and Columcille. On Station Island one of the penitential beds bears her name, and a Cross of St. Brigid, inscribed in stone, is the focal point of one of the pilgrimage rites there. Along the south shore of Lough Derg we find both a St. Brigid's Chair and a St. Brigid's Well, natural features linked to her name.

Although there are biographies, one at least dating from the seventh century, her story is full of conflicting details and obvious legend. She was born c.451, probably near Dundalk in Louth. She became a nun and founded religious institutions, most famously, around 470, the double monastery of Kildare Abbey. She died around 525. Her feast day is February 1, and her relics are revered at Downpatrick.

St. Catherine.

The identity of this Catherine, whose penitential bed is one of six on Station Island, is almost certainly the fourth-century Catherine of Alexandria — a virgin-martyr, poet and scholar. Her tremendous popularity during the Middle Ages was ignited by the discovery of her tomb on Mount Sinai around 800. She is particularly associated with pilgrimage, since Mount Sinai and other sites associated with her relics —Rouen and Canterbury, for example — attracted many pilgrims. Her feast day is November 24/25, but her life is mostly a matter of legend.

St. Dabheoc. (Also Dabeocus, Davog, Beoanus, Bioc, Beoan, Aedh, Hugh.)

St. Dabheoc is the one saint physically connected with Lough Derg. His history is full of competing and complimentary legends; and indeed there were probably at least two Dabheocs confused and conflated over time, and perhaps both of them were in residence at Lough Derg.

One was a contemporary of Patrick; the other dates from the seventh century. While the later

Dabheoc may have been a relative of Patrick's first convert, Dichu, and from Down, the lineage and birthplace of the earlier one, the son of Brecan, are associated with Wales. The fifth-century saint predicted the birth, virtues and sanctity of St. Columcille, who was born in 521. The tenth-century *Martyrology of Tallaght* mentions Aedh of Lough Gierg (an alternative word for "derg"), who was most likely the later saint. In any case the Dabheoc who lent his name to various monuments in the area of Lough Derg was an anchorite who apparently lived on one of the Lough Derg islands with a community of other anchoritic men.

Places bearing his name include St. Dabheoc's Chair on the south bank of Lough Derg. The chair is partially a natural crag, to which large blocks were added, and probably a Bronze Age burial site. In addition to the chair, there is also on Station Island a bed, or the remains of a beehive hut, which embraces both Dabheoc and Molaise. Nearby Seavadog Mountain is in the townland of Seedavoc (St. Dabheoc's Seat). It is also possible that Saints Island was originally named St. Dabheoc's Island, although this may have been another island entirely, which also may have contained his tomb. The plunder of the Termon Dabheoc is mentioned in the *Annals of Ulster* for 1070; and the *Annals of the Four Masters* mentions the same for 1111.

It appears that Lough Derg may indeed have originally been a pilgrimage site frequented because of Dabheoc, and that the reputation of the site was appropriated and popularized in the name of Patrick in the twelfth century by the Augustinians who inherited the site.

Dabheoc's feast days include October 26 or 28, but other days also associated with the Dabheocs are January 1, July 24, and December 15 and 16.

St. Malachy. (Also Máel Máedóc Ua Norgair, Maelmhaedhoc Ó Morgair.)

St. Malachy is one of the latest saints associated with the Pilgrim's Way to Lough Derg. He is not venerated there, nor at any of the points along the way to Lough Derg, but he may have done more than any single other saint to establish and promote this pilgrimage. He brought the church in Ireland under Roman rules and imposed some regularity on its structures. He also introduced the Augustinian Canons into Ireland in the 1140s and put the monastery at Lough Derg under their rule. Many towns along the route — Dublin, Devenish, Drumlane and Kells — had Augustinian churches. After meeting Bernard of Clairvaux, he later introduced the Cistercian order into Ireland and those churches also created part of the network of support for pilgrims: St. Mary's Abbey in Dublin, the great abbey at Mellifont and St. Peter and Paul at Armagh: some pilgrims record detouring to Armagh to obtain permission to enter St. Patrick's Purgatory. H. of Saltrey, author of the *Tractatus de Purgatorio Sancti Patricii,* the first surviving written account of St. Patick's Purgatory, was of this same order.

Born in 1094, Malachy died in November 2, 1148 at Clairvaux in the company of St. Bernard, who later wrote a life of this Irish bishop. Malachy's feast day is celebrated on November 3. He was the first Irish saint canonized by Rome (1199).

ST. PATRICK. (Also Pádraig.)

St. Patrick, the patron saint of Ireland — or one of the three patrons saints of Ireland with Brigid and Columcille — is closely identified with the Pilgrim's Way to Lough Derg, since the end point of this journey is the Purgatory of St. Patrick. The staring point of the journey — St. Patrick's Cathedral, Dublin — is, however, more positively tied to Patrick, since it was apparently built on the site where he reportedly baptized converts to Christianity.

Several later biographies of Patrick have come down to us, but his life is shrouded in mystery and legend. Two of his letters provide the only details of his life that are considered factual: he was born c.387 in Banna Venta Berniae (possibly in Cumbria), the son of a Romano–British deacon. At the age of fourteen, Patrick was kidnapped from Britain by a troop of Irish invaders, and he remained in Ireland for six years. He escaped and returned to his family, entered the church, eventually becoming a bishop. He returned to Ireland and although it is not certain, he seems to have worked principally in the north and west (Mayo) converting the Irish to Christianity. The date of his death is generally accepted as 493, and many believe that the date of his death corresponds to his feast day: March 17. His remains are said to be preserved at Downpatrick along with those of Brigid and Columcille, but there is no certainty regarding this.

Patrick's connection with Lough Derg may indeed be a twelfth-century revision. St. Malachy and the Augustinians may have attached his name to the site and helped to develop the legend of St. Patrick's Purgatory, replacing the local St. Dabheoc with a renowned figure capable of drawing more-than-insular attention. The promotion of a pilgrimage site in that region may also be the result of rivalries among dioceses growing out of the Synod of Kells (1152). However, without more solid documentation, this all remains conjecture (Pontfarcy, 32–33).

It is certain that a legend grew up around this same time concerning Lough Derg and Patrick, attributing to him the slaying of the devil's mother, Coara (also Corra, Cornu, Caorthannach) — a demon bird, formed like a black heron with no feathers, except for four or five on her wings — whose blood turned the lake red ("derg"). Another version of this same story claims that the monster is not dead but was persuaded to stay at the bottom of the lake until La Luain, which she thought was Monday, but was really to be the apocalyptic Last Day.

There is also the legend about the *purgatorium* that has associated St. Patrick with Station Island: when Patrick was trying to convert the Irish, they wanted a sign and when Patrick prayed to God for such a sign, and He revealed to him a cave through which one could enter the otherworld and view the punishments of hell and the joys of heaven.

RELIGIOUS ORDERS

In 1130 or 1134, the Canons Regular of St. Augustine were in control of Lough Derg as a dependent priory of Sts. Peter and Paul in Armagh. It remained in the hands of the canons, even after the suppression in 1632, since the lay owner of the property permitted the canons to remain. Franciscans arrived in 1710 and were fully established here by 1763. From 1785 the diocese of Clogher appointed secular priests to administer the establishment.

BUILDINGS OF THE PAST

No remains of the original buildings on either Saints or Station Islands are uncovered, and there are presently no buildings at all on Saints Island. Apparently neither site has ever been excavated, except for an attempt in 1693 by Ludovicus Pyrhus of Brittany. Any medieval buildings on either island were destroyed in 1632, but several descriptions survive and most agree with one another.

Map: OS 11

Parking: Parking is available on the mainland at the Visitors Centre.

Paths and Trails: In addition to the Pilgrims's Path to Saints Island described below (pp. 141–43) additional trails are sheltered in this area, some more and some less evident: one from Castlederg through Killeter, now part of the National Cycle Network, eventually joining the road from Pettigo to Lough Derg just below Tawlaght (app. 27 k/16.8 mi long); a route from Kiltierney (where in a field are the inaccessible remains of a grange) over Drumawark (= the hill of the view) where the "Millennium Cross" of 1999 replaces an older termon (or boundary) cross (app. 15.3 k/9.5 mi long); and a route from Donegal past Aughkeen Mountain to Donegal Point on Lough Derg (app. 13.2 k/8.2 mi long).

Amenities: Full facilities are available on Station Island for those on pilgrimage; at the Visitor Centre there are toilets; otherwise the nearest facilities are at Pettigo (7 k/4.3 mi S).

Saints Island.

SAINTS ISLAND

History: According to legend, the monastery on Saints Island was founded by St. Patrick or by St. Dabheoc in the time of Patrick, with Dabheoc presiding. In 1130 or 1134, under the probable influence of St. Malachy, the monastery became a priory of Augustinian Canons under the cathedral of Sts. Peter and Paul in Armagh; Arrouaise after 1140. It was plundered in the late twelfth and early thirteenth centuries.

Remains: An Ordnance Survey map from the nineteenth century shows Saints Island as it appears today: roundish, but wider than tall. It also indicates an enclosing wall almost directly in the center of the island with a graveyard to the southeast. On the northeast shore is an old quay and to the southeast of the island there is indication of stone piers for an ancient wooden bridge connecting to the mainland. This same map, however, also indicates "Purgatory" toward the northeast corner of this island.

While Saints Island is not fully described in any surviving text, a few fifteenth-century accounts mention the priory and one mentions a cloister as well. A later text mentions a graveyard.

The Pilgrims Path to Saints Island, from behind the statue of St. Patrick as a young pilgrim near the Visitors Centre, passes St. Brigid's Chair (probably a natural feature inexplicably associated with the saint), St. Dabheoc's Chair (possibly a bronze-age burial site) and St. Brigid's Well (marked by a modern cross covered with pilgrims' votive rags).

Access: The Pilgrims Path is marked from behind the Visitor Centre to Saints Island across land managed by Coillte, the Irish Forestry organisation. At about St. Brigid's Well, the Pilgrims Path joins the medieval pilgrims road, which arrives here from Pettigo through Templecarne (Carn). There is no access to the island itself, but a clear view from the trail over

Along the Pilgrims Path, Lough Derg.

the recently cut woods. Saints Island has never been excavated. The total distance of the circuit path is an easy 12 k (7 mi).

Italica Picture Gallery:
http://gallery.me.com/egardiner#100384

Online References:
http://www.heritagecouncil.ie/recreation/heritage-council-initiatives/the-pilgrim-paths/lough-derg/
http://www.donegaldirect.ie/Uploads/Documents/File_1663_LoughDergMapA4.pdf
http://www.pettigo.com
http://www.triskelle.eu/attractions/loughderg.php

Bibliography:
Cunningham (1984).
Cunningham (2007), 21, 22.
Gwynn & Hadcock, 193.
Harbison & Lynam (2004).
Haren & de Pontfarcy (1988).
Flynn (1984).
McGuinness (2000).
Rowan, 406-8.
http://www.hell-on-line.org/BibPatrick.html

STATION ISLAND / ST. PATRICK'S PURGATORY

History: In c.1100 a monastery on Saints Island was associated with the smaller Station Island, and by 1135 the Augustinian Canons were in place here. In 1146/7, Owein, a knight from Britain, visited the Purgatory, and his experience was recounted in the *Tractatus de Purgatorio Sancti Patricii,* which is widely credited with spawning a literature about, and pilgrimages to, Lough Derg.

The first detailed map of the island dates to 1666, from the book *Lyra Hibernica* by Fr. Thomas Carve. Although it places Lough Derg in County Tyrone, it agrees with written descriptions. Oriented so that north is near the bottom–right corner of the map, it shows the "templum" or St. Patrick's Chapel at the south, with the Purgatory northeast of it and the penitential beds northwest of that, even showing early evidence for the bed of St. Catherine.

The nineteenth-century Ordnance Survey map mentioned above (p. 141) shows Station Island as two joined forms: at top an ovoid tilting slightly to the west narrowly connected at its base to a triangle that swings off to the east. Among the structures shown are (clockwise from top right): a lodging house, a wine boiler, the six penitential beds, the Confessional or St. Mary's Chapel, the landing place, the priest's house, lodging houses, St. Patrick's Cross and St. Patrick's Chapel.

Station Island is described by eye-witnesses in several texts, which often note that the island is separated into two parts, although some go on to say that one part is overgrown and inhabited by demons and the other is covered by proper trees and inhabited by angels. They mention the chapel of St. Patrick, which was in the southwest corner and also beehive huts, cells or penitential beds of varying numbers near the chapel. Guillebert de Lannoy (1430) describes them as four or five wattle huts covered with thatch;

Map of Station Island from *Lyra Hibernica*, 1666.

Francesco Chiericati (1517) mentions three: those of Brigid, Patrick and Columcille; the 1630 *Martyrology of Donegal* mentions five beds of hard penance (Patrick, Columcille, Brigid, Adamnan and Dabheoc).

More texts describe the cave itself, and here most agree as well. Guillebert de Lannoy left the most detailed description:

> The site of St. Patrick's Purgatory is like a Flemish window well-locked and of a single roof and is as high as the earth of the Chapel and faces North at four paces near the North-East corner from it in a direct line from the corner aforesaid. And the Hole is nine feet long from East to West and then turns five feet towards the South-West and as a whole is fourteen to fifteen feet long. It is built with black stones and is about two feet wide and three feet high and at the end of this Hole…they say is a mouth of Hell but St. Patrick stopped it with a stone which he placed there which is there yet. (Leslie, 39.)

Most of these details concerning the Purgatory are confirmed by the other surviving texts where, in translation, it is variously referred to as a cave, a cellar, or an enclosed pit. It was slightly to the northeast of the early chapel and had a locked door or gate. The entrance was quite narrow: about half a meter (2 ft) wide and 1 m (3 ft) high. It descended slightly downward: there seems to have been perhaps six steps. This part of the cave seems to have measured about 3 m (9 ft) long. It was covered with stones so low that there was only height enough to kneel. One text indicates that the sides of the cave may have been banked.

After this there was a turn: Ramon de Perellós (1397) says towards the left; but Guillebert's and Mannini's descriptions indicate that the turn might be towards the right. This turning seems to have created

Three Penitential Beds, Bell Tower (above Site of St. Patrick's Purgatory) and St. Mary's Chapel, Station Island.

a niche about 5 feet long. George Grissaphan claims that he entered the cave from the church and that the cave was two miles long, but his account, which was recorded by an anonymous compiler some time after the event, is inconsistent with the others.

The cave could hold several people, some texts say five or six, others as many as fourteen. Pilgrims do mention being inside with others, and one pilgrim mentions that when there were too many to fit inside the cave, they were locked in the chapel for the night, which is obviously the origin of the "Prison" Chapel and most likely of the current practice of the overnight vigil in the church.

It has been suggested that the cave was probably the site of an ancient souterrain, but the description also matches ancient sweat houses, which are found throughout Ireland, and in some parts were still being used into the twentieth century. These stone-covered caves had small entrances and could fit, on seats along the wall, three or four people who would spend several hours inside. They were filled with a healing or purging smoke — some say a smoke that created visions and hallucinations. The niche at the turning of the cave may have been an addition to a sweat house, but without excavations this remains tantalizing conjecture.

A major curiosity in the history of St. Patrick's Purgatory is the Italian fresco of c.1346 in the Convent of S. Francesco, Todi. This is clearly not considered an accurate rendering of the cave but shows a small hill, similar to the one on Station Island. It now has six

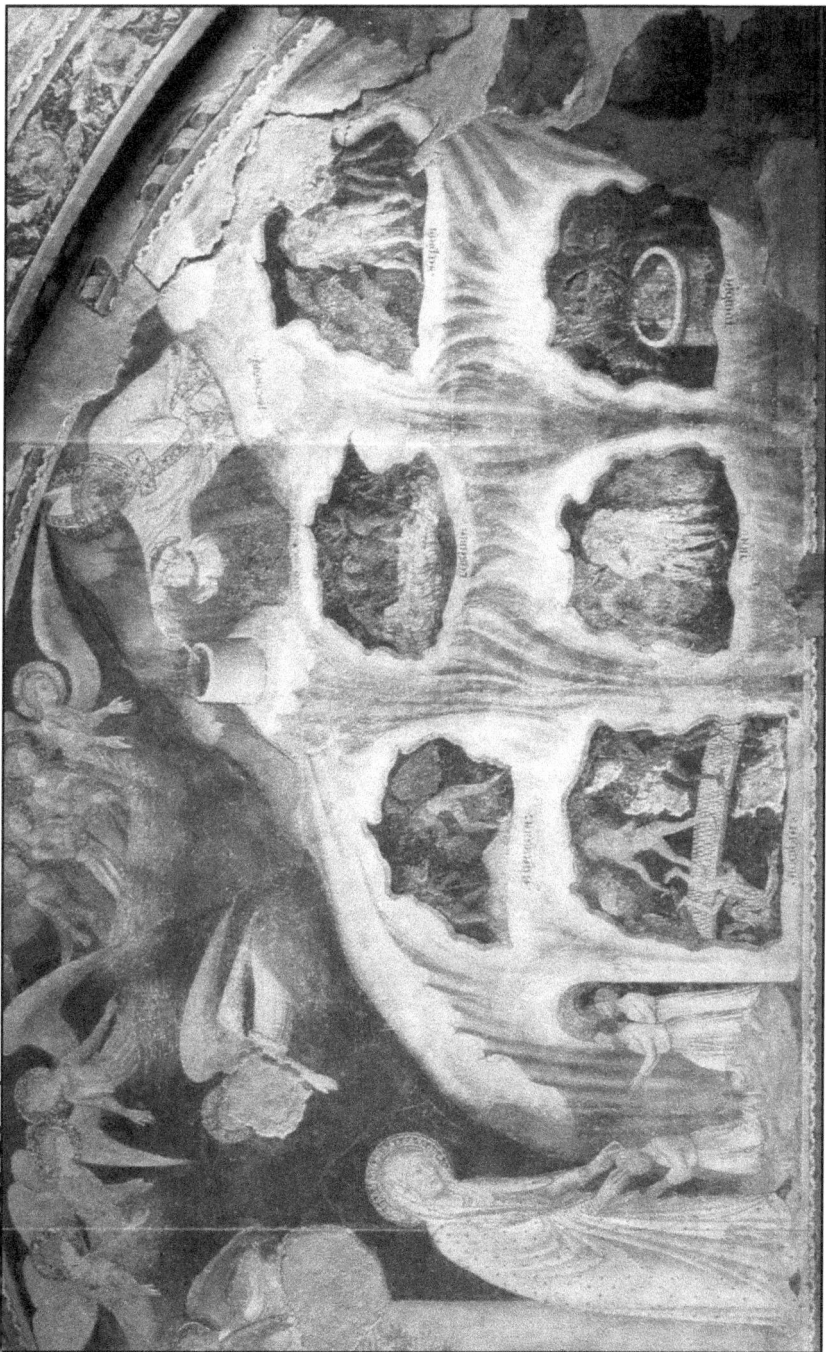

St. Patrick's Purgatory, Fresco, detail, Todi.

chambers, each marked with the Latin names for six of the seven deadly sins: avarice, lust, pride, envy, anger and sloth. The rendering of the seventh chamber, for gluttons, has been badly damaged and would be in the far lower right corner. St. Patrick and a figure not conclusively labeled as Lord Nicholas seem to be inspecting the chimney. Nicholas has been associated with both St. Nicholas and a certain Nicholas the pilgrim, perhaps the one whose visit is described in the *Golden Legend* of Jacobus de Voraigne, who may have been conflated with Owein. A female saint at the portal welcomes the purged sinners. She has been identified as the Madonna della Consolazione (or Virgin of Mercy), a popular iconographic type — particularly in Italy — which interpreted Mary as an intercessor for human souls. The fresco continues to the left where the souls are welcomed into heaven (Mac Tréinfhir, 155).

CURRENT BUILDINGS ON STATION ISLAND

The Franciscans built a friary on Station Island in 1763, called St. Mary of the Angels. It was rebuilt in 1813 and 1870 and in 2003 underwent restoration to its 1860 construction. St. Patrick's Basilica, also referred to as the Prison Chapel, was built in 1780. A new church of the same name was finished in 1929. A large hospice — now called the men's hospice — was built in 1880. In 1910–12, a women's hospice was built off the shoulder of the island on the lake bed. This was demolished in 2000 to make way for Davog House, a retreat center named for St. Dabheoc. This is now the latest building on the island, completed in 2005. There is also a shop with books and other items.

There are six penitential beds, the remains of early beehive cells or oratories, dedicated to seven saints. They include, clockwise from the northernmost, the beds of St. Brigid, St. Catherine of Alexandria, St. Columcille, St. Patrick, St. Molaise and St. Dabheoc,

Station Island: 1. St. Patrick's Basilica; 2. Flood Room; 3. Cloak Room; 4. Davog House; 5. Labyrinth; 6. Penitential Beds; 7. St. Mary's Chapel; 8. Shop; 9. Landing Dock; 10. Staff House; 11. Dining Room; 12. Women's Dormitory; 13. Reception; 14. Men's Dormitory; 15. Site of Cave.

151

and St. Brendan. A ninth-century column that now supports a small cross, St. Patrick's Cross, was probably once surmounted by a stone cross.

Southeast of the beds a bell tower is perched on a mound, and the entrance to the purgatory would have been, most likely, in the north side of this mound. Today it is completely overgrown and nothing marks the exact location.

Reliquary, St. Mary's Chapel, Station Island.

Relics: In the basilica there is a large reliquary of the True Cross; in St. Mary's Chapel, an ornate, modern reliquary containing the relics of almost 30 saints, including such early Irish saints as Malachy, Killian, Frigidian and Patrick, but these relics all came to Lough Derg during the modern period.

An account of an excavation in 1693 (O'Connor, *Lough Derg,* 130–31), mentions a square bronze bell, identified as St. Dabheoc's Bell, which was kept on the altar on Station Island, and which is now missing, although there was rumor of such a bell in the collection of Trinity College, Dublin.

Another bell, identified as St. Patrick's Bell by Míchaél Ó Cléirigh (c.1600), was at that time already

St. Patrick's Bell.
© The Trustees of the National Museums of Scotland.

in three fragments and may be the same as one from the John Bell collection, now in the National Museum of Scotland (although presently not on display).

Italica Picture Gallery:
http://gallery.me.com/ egardiner#100399

Online References:
http://www.loughderg.org/
http://www.clogherdiocese .ie/lough-derg
http://www.hell-on-line.org/TextsJC.html#Patrick

Bibliography:
Cunningham (1984).
Flynn (1984).
Haren & de Pontfarcy (1988).
McGuinness (2000).
Rowan, 406-8.
http://www.hell-on-line.org/BibPatrick.html

Access: Access to Station Island is restricted and is possible only by boat and only during the pilgrimage season (from early June to mid-August).

If you intend to take part in the physical and spiritual challenge on Station Island, you'll certainly want to obtain up-to-date information directly from Lough Derg (http://www.loughderg.org). A few details here, however, might be useful.

For the three-day pilgrimage it is possible to arrive any morning during the season at the Visitor Centre on the mainland. However, this is a penitential pilgrimage with a continuous cycle of prayer and meditation. Pilgrims need to fast from midnight of the night before they arrive at Lough Derg. Boats depart for Station Island in the morning, starting around 10:00, and you will spend two nights on the island: the first night in the basilica in vigil, without sleep. Your only meals — of dry toast and black tea or coffee — will be served once on each day. After you depart on the third morning, you will need to keep your fast until midnight.

Although the liturgy and rituals are Roman Catholic, the pilgrimage is open and welcoming to people of all faiths and none. The only distinction is made in the sacramental rites: although non-Catholics join in the celebration of Mass, they do not receive communion; and while they also join in the celebration of reconciliation and are invited to speak with a priest, they do not necessarily "confess." Pilgrims must be at least fifteen years of age.

A one-day pilgrimage is also available, but this is more restricted and available only to individuals unable for physical reasons to take part in the 3-day pilgrimage.

APPENDIX 1.
A TAXONOMY OF PILGRIMAGE

This following chart compares Lough Derg with Rome, Santiago de Compostela and Jerusalem on fourteen specific points outlined in the taxonomy presented in Chapter 2 (above, pp. 5–19). This comparison presents evidence of how the Pilgrim's Way to St. Patrick's Purgatory conforms to a standard for medieval pilgrimage sites.

Elements of the Major Christian Pilgrimage Routes	Rome	Jerusalem
Cult Site	St. Peter's Basilica	Holy Sepulchre
Saint/ Principal Cult Figure	St. Peter	Jesus
Secondary Cult Figures	Saints Paul, Mary, Lawrence, John the Baptist and John the Evangelist, Bartholomew, Stephen (all represented by major basilicas), among others.	Mary, St. Anne, the Apostles, Hebrew Bible figures, and numerous others.
Principal Route	The Via Francigena, based on the itinerary of Sigeric the Serious, archbishop of Canterbury, leads from there across France, Switzerland and Italy where at Aosta it is joined by other routes and heads south to Rome.	Pilgrims would usually sail from Brindisi or Venice and arrive in Haifa.
Alternate Routes	Alternate routes brought pilgrims by ship from Genoa and Barcelona, or overland from Spain and southern France as well as from Brindisi and other southern Italian cities.	Pilgrims could actually sail from perhaps any port on the Mediterranean to Haifa and then overland to Jerusalem. Land routes existed that led from Europe across the Balkans and Asia Minor.

APPENDIX 1. A TAXONOMY OF PILGRIMAGE

Santiago de Compostela	Lough Derg
Cathedral of St. James	St. Patrick's Purgatory
St. James	St. Patrick is now considered the principle cult figure, but he is a high-profile saint who in the 12th century probably displaced the earlier — and local — Donegal saint here, St. Dabheoc.
Twenty-five saints are mentioned in connection with the "Pilgrim's Guide" alone. These range, for example, from St. Hilary at Poitiers and St. Martin at Tours, to St. Honoratus at Arles, St. Saturninus at Toulouse, and St. Leonard at Noblat.	Saints Dabheoc, Brendan, Brigid, Columcille, Molaise and Catherine of Alexandria are associated with Station Island in particular, while along the route the following saints are also in evidence: St. Cassán, St. Ciarán, St. Erc, St. Feidhlimidh, St. Mac Cuilinn, St. Maedhóg, St. Malachy, St. Nennid and St. Ronan.
The Way of St. James comprises a wide variety of routes, including the Camino Frances, Via Lemovicensis, Via Podiensis, Via Turonensis and the Via Tolosana, which converged at two main spots — Jaca and Roncevaux in the Pyrenees — where the route led across northern Spain to Compostela.	There is an identifiable route to St. Patrick's Purgatory that follows old roads like the Dublin Road, as well as waterways. It traveled from Dublin north to Drogheda, and there turned west and north up the Boyne and Blackwater Valleys into the Lough Erne region, and into Donegal. The particulars of this route are attested to by Guillebert de Lannoy (1430).
From Mounts' Bay in Cornwall or Plymouth in Devon by ship to La Coruña; overland from Bilbao, Madrid, Seville (Via de la Plata), Barcelona and Lisbon.	From Dublin or Downpatrick through Armagh and Clogher. These alternate routes were mentioned in 1397 (Ramon de Perellós) and 1517 (Francesco Chiericati). From Donegal to Lough Derg, and no doubt from the south, perhaps from Limerick up the Shannon into Lough Erne.

Elements of the Major Christian Pilgrimage Routes	Rome	Jerusalem
Stations	The route from Canterbury to Rome, as we know it today, would include stops at: Bruay, Arras, Reims, Châlons-sur-Marne, Bar-sur-Aube, Langres, Besançon, Pontarlier, Lausanne and Saint-Maurice, then travel over the Great St. Bernard Pass to Aosta, Ivrea, Vercelli, Pavia, Fidenza, Aulla, Luni, Lucca, Poggibonsi, Siena, San Quirico, Bolsena, Viterbo and Sutri before Rome.	Sailing from Venice or Brindisi and arriving in the Holy Land, stops would include Tyre, Acre, Haifa, Tiberias, Sea of Galilee, Nazareth, Jordan River, Jericho, Mount Tabor, Bethany, Bethlehem.
Relics	Rome contained the remains of Saints Peter and Paul, and numerous other Apostles and early saints and martyrs. The "Stacyons of Rome" listed the relics and indulgences at various Roman churches.	The principal relic was the Tomb of Christ, but Jerusalem is replete with other relics of Jesus, Mary and the Apostles. Theoderich of Wurzbürg (c.1172) and Richard Torkington (1517) mention the many relics exhibited in the Holy Land.
Emblems/ Tokens/ Mementos	The Keys of St. Peter and the "Vera" Icon (image of the face of Jesus) were major emblems for Rome, and were generally cast in pewter or lead and worn as a badge. Early mementos also included phials of oil from the catacombs or wax Agnus Dei's.	The palm leaf, a phial with water from the Jordan, and the Cross of Jerusalem were typical emblems from the Holy Land.

Santiago de Compostela	Lough Derg
In addition to the numerous stations in France from Amiens to Vezelay, in Spain there would be stops at Jaca or Roncevaux/ Pamplona, Eunate, Puente la Reina, Logroño, Burgos, Fromista, Carrion de los Condes, Sahagun, San Miguel de la Escalada, Leon, Astorga, Ponferrada, Villafranca del Bierzo, O Cebreiro, Tricastela, Sarria, Portomarin.	The stations between Dublin and St. Patrick's Purgatory include: Swords, Lusk, Drogheda, Mellifont, Slane, Donaghmore, Kells, Castlekeeran, Kilmore, Drumlane, Aghalurcher, Devenish, Inishmacsaint and White Island.
The principal relic was the body of St. James, which, according to one legend, miraculously appeared in Galicia after being transported over the seas from the Holy Land in a stone boat.	There is some evidence for bell relics and a relic of the True Cross. It was probably the resting place of the remains of St. Dabheoc and other holy men and may also have had other relics translated there in the 12th century. Many other relics have been identified along the route to Lough Derg, and often they are now in museums, although many more have been lost or are presently unaccounted for.
The scallop shell, which could be collected from the shores of Galicia, was the emblem of Compostela and eventually became a symbol throughout Europe for pilgrimage.	The token associated with St. Patrick's Purgatory is the penal crucifix: a small carved wooden cross with a ring at the top for attaching it around the neck by a cord. Mention of a cross in connection with this pilgrimage dates from as early as 1353 and 1411. The earliest physical example dates from 1702.

Elements of the Major Christian Pilgrimage Routes	Rome	Jerusalem
Rites and Rituals	In Rome by the early 13th century, pilgrims were enjoined to visit the stational churches, in each of which the pope would say Mass on an appointed day — usually during the 40 days of Lent. At the end of this round of ceremonial church-going the promised indulgences would be conferred on pilgrims who completed the requirements.	Pilgrims would follow the life of Christ at the various holy sites especially during Holy Week. This is the original of the post-Tridentine "Stations of the Cross." A 15th-century description includes Latin prayers to be said at various sites.
Motivations: Penance and Petitions	A certain Rathbert c.870 was sent on several pilgrimages, including one to Rome, for battering his mother to death. Peter Damian, the eleventh-century reformer and saint, sent the corrupt Milanese clergy on pilgrimage to Rome. In 1319 Roger of Bonito was sent on pilgrimage to Rome (as well as Santiago de Compostela and Jerusalem) for murdering the bishop of Frigento, Avellino. Other examples abound.	Evidence includes Ejegod, a 9th-century Dane, and Fulk Nerra, the count of Anjou in the 10th century, who made penitential pilgrimages to the Holy Land. As late as the late 16th century Shakespeare has Henry IV declare his intention to make a pilgrimage to the Holy Land to atone for his sins. Modern historiography generally agrees that the Crusades incorporated the penitential pilgrimage in its motivation.
Expectations: Indulgences and Miracles	Visiting the tombs of the Apostles in Rome, especially along the established Stations, was the most important source of indulgence in Europe. Giovanni Villani offers detailed evidence of the 1300 Jubilee Pilgrimage and its indulgences. By the 15th century the guidebooks to Rome, such as John Capgrave's, incorporated the indulgences attached to each site. The "Stacyons of Rome" listed the indulgences at various Roman churches. Gerald of Wales (c.1200) visited Rome as a pilgrim and amassed 92 years of indulgences after attending 395 masses.	Pilgrims or crusaders to Jerusalem, from the time of the preaching of the First Crusade in 1095, would be rewarded with indulgences. Simone Sigoli (1384), Arnold von Harff (1496–99), and the 15th-century *Information for Pilgrims unto the Holy Land* include detailed listings of indulgences.

Santiago de Compostela	Lough Derg
Upon arriving in Compostela, pilgrims would spend a night of fasting just outside or inside the cathedral, and the following morning participate in a series of rituals and offerings before being awarded their indulgence.	The pilgrimage at St. Patrick's Purgatory once involved long rituals of prayer and fasting before a pilgrim was permitted to spend a night in the cave on Station Island. After the cave was closed in the 17th century, fasting and prayers and the rounds of the penitential beds have remained integral parts of the pilgrimage rite.
In a 9th-century story recorded in *The Miracles of St. James,* a sinner from Italy was told to write his sin on a piece of paper and take it to St. James to seek forgiveness. George Grissaphan, a knight of Hungary who took part in the invasion of Naples with King Lewis in 1347/8 walked from Avignon to Santiago de Compostela to repent for the murders he committed as a knight.	From the earliest account of the Knight Owein, the pilgrimage to St. Patrick's Purgatory was undertaken to atone for sins; and George Grissaphan a knight of Hungary visited Lough Derg in 1353 to atone for crimes that he committed as a knight. But more than any other site, Lough Derg is, by its very nature, associated with penance.
Shrines, such as Compostela, involved the commutation of punishments both earthly and otherworldly. Legend has it that in 1122 Pope Calixtus II endowed Compostela with the privilege of granting a plenary indulgence in jubilee years — when the saint's day, 25 July, fell on a Sunday. The earliest document for this indulgence dates from the mid-13th century.	Many early texts assert that if anyone endures this place in a spirit of penance he would never suffer the pains of hell. A document of 12 August 1507 by Master Donatus Magrahe, prior of St. Patrick's Purgatory, mentions a share "in all the indulgences of divers Roman pontiffs and other bishops, namely 10,670 years granted to our place." Even today a popular legend claims that three visits to Lough Derg will save any pilgrim from hell.

Elements of the Major Christian Pilgrimage Routes	Rome	Jerusalem
Early Record	The pilgrimage to Rome is quite early, dating to the 3rd century, with the earliest record dating from 725. Archbishop Sigeric laid out an itinerary for the trip to Rome from Canterbury in the later 10th century.	The earliest surviving document for the Holy Land pilgrimage is 386: Paula and Eustochium's "Letter to Marcella on the Holy Places."
Literary Tradition	For Rome there were works such as the *Einseideln Itinerary* of the late 8th/early 9th century, the *Mirabilia urbis Romae* of the 12th century and the *Graphia aureae urbis Romae* of the 13th or 14th century.	The Palestine Pilgrims Text Society published 13 volumes, which include over 30 accounts dating from the 4th to the 15th century for the Holy Land.
Cultural Memory	Rome has from antiquity enjoyed a rich status that is evidenced by the terms long applied to it like "The City (Urbs)" and "The Eternal City." Before it became a destination for Christians, it was already a destination for the world.	A longing to visit the places that Christ walked helped to fill the ranks of pilgrims to the Holy Land from before the 5th century. In addition to being a Christian destination, it is a holy place for Muslims and Jews, as well.

APPENDIX 1. A TAXONOMY OF PILGRIMAGE

Santiago de Compostela	Lough Derg
For Compostela the pilgrimage may be as early as 814, but the earliest record of the route dates from the 12th century.	Although Keating's 17th-century *History of Ireland* mentions a 1170 reference to St. Patrick's Purgatory, the earliest certain mention of the site dates from 1185 in the *Tractatus de Purgatorio Sanctii Patricii*. Guillebert de Lannoy (1430) attested to this route.
The 12th-century Codex Calixtinus or *Liber sancti Jacobi* and *Historia Compostelana* on the reign of Diego Gelmirez are texts associated with this site. William Wey (1456) and Hieronymus Münzer (1494/5) also left written accounts of their journeys to Santiago de Compostela.	The literary tradition for the pilgrimage to St. Patrick's Purgatory is enormous, beginning with the *Tractatus de Purgatorio Sanctii Patricii* (1185), and including medieval accounts by pilgrims from Spain, France, Hungary, Italy, Germany and England. (See http://www.hell-on-line.org/BibPatrick.html)
From the 8th or 9th century, Santiago de Compostela enticed thousands of pilgrims from all across Europe annually to pray at the saint's tomb.	When St. Patrick's Purgatory first appears in the literature it already is a full-blown pilgrimage destination and, despite its closure in 1632, pilgrims apparently never ceased to visit this site from the days of St. Dabheoc.

Drumlane Abbey.

APPENDIX 2.
CHRONOLOGY

100 c.e.	Ptolemy records sixteen tribes in Ireland.
387 (c.)	St. Patrick born.
391 (c.)	St. Patrick kidnapped to Ireland.
4th C.	St. Catherine of Alexandria fl.
433	St. Patrick baptized the townspeople of Drogheda at a well. St. Patrick built a fire on the Hill of Slane.
445	*Senchús Mor,* penitential.
451 (c.)	St. Brigid born.
470	St. Finián of Clonard born.
470 (c.)	St. Brigid founds monastery at Kildare.
484 (c.)	St. Brendan born.
493	St. Patrick dies, possibly March 17.
493 (post)	Slane Abbey founded.
498 (ante)	Lusk Monastery founded by St. Mac Cuilinn.
496/8	Sept. 6, St. Mac Cuilinn dies.
5th C.	St. Cassán fl.
512	St. Brendan ordained a priest.
513/4	St. Erc dies.
521	Dec. 7, St. Columcille born.
530 (ante)	Inishmacsaint founded by St. Nennid.
523/30	St. Nennid dies.
525 (c.)	St. Brigid dies.
534	St. Ciarán of Clonmacnoise visits Inishmacsaint.
549	St. Finián of Clonard dies.
550	Drumlane Abbey, possibly founded by Columcille, already flourishing.
550 (c.)	St. Columcille founds abbeys at Kells and Drumlane.
6th C. (early)	Monastery of Swords founded by St. Columcille.
555/58/60	St. Maedhóg born.
563	St. Columcille exiles himself to northern Scotland.
564 (ante)	Devenish Monastery founded by St. Molaise.
564	St. Molaise dies.
577	St. Brendan dies.
597	June 9, St. Columcille dies at Iona.
598	St. Maedhóg elected bishop of Ferns in Wexford.
6th C. late	Drumlane Abbey restored by St. Maedhóg.
625/26/32	St. Maedhóg dies.

6ᵗʰ/7ᵗʰ C.	Aghalurcher Monastery established by St. Ronan. St. Feidhlimidh founds Kilmore Monastery.
778 (ante)	St. Ciarán's abbey founded.
770/78	St. Ciarán dies, possibly June 14, 775.
8ᵗʰ C.	*Collectio canonum Hibernensis,* penitential.
800 (c.)	Body of St. Catherine of Alexandria discovered at Mount Sinai. Book of Kells produced. *Old Irish Penitential.*
802	Iona burned by Norsemen.
804 (c.)	Monks of Iona flee Viking raids to Kells and establish a monastery.
806	Vikings kill 68 monks at Iona.
807	Church of Columcille at Kells destroyed.
827	Lusk plundered by Vikings.
833	Slane Abbey plundered.
840	Staff Shrine of Feidhlimidh mentioned in the *Annals of Ireland.*
849	Drogheda raided and burned by Vikings.
850	*St. Hubert Penitential.*
856	Lusk plundered by Vikings.
875	*Annals of Ireland* mentions the shrine of Columcille, possibly a tomb-shaped reliquary, brought to Ireland.
877	Reliquaries of Columcille transferred to Kells.
9ᵗʰ C.	Aghalurcher Monastery dedicated to St. Ronan.
919	Kells Abbey plundered by Vikings.
948	Staff shrine and bell shrine of St. Erc recorded in the *Annals of Ireland.*
949	Castlekeeran plundered by Norsemen.
950	Kells Abbey plundered by Vikings. Slane Abbey belfry burned.
969	Kells Abbey plundered by Vikings.
994	Monastery at Swords burned.
9ᵗʰ/10ᵗʰ C.	St. Columcille's House built, presumably to shelter his remains.
1000 (c.)	*Irish Canons from a Worcester Collection,* penitential.
1006/7	Book of Kells and shrine stolen; shrine never recovered.
1019	Kells Abbey plundered.
1020–1166	Monastery of Swords burned and plundered several times.
1028	Slane Abbey oratory collapsed.
1034	*Annals of Ireland* mentions the bed of Columcille lost at sea.

1038 (c.)	Church or priory of the Holy Trinity, later known as Christ Church Cathedral, Dublin, founded.
1047	Cuduilig, erenach of Kells, dies.
1053	Lusk plundered.
1070	*Annals of Ulster* mentions the plundering of Termon Dabheoc.
1089	Lusk plundered by men of Munster.
1094	St. Malachy born.
1100 (c.)	Monastery on Saints Island, associated with Station Island.
1111	Synod of Rathbreasail. Kells Abbey burned by the Irish. *Annals of the Four Masters* mentions the plundering of Termon Dabheoc.
1121	Earliest evidence for church on site of St. Patrick's, Dublin.
1127	*Annals of Ireland* mentions the shrine of Columcille, probably a tomb-shaped reliquary.
1130	Abbey Church of St. Mary founded on Devenish.
1130/34	Canons Regular of St. Augustine in control of Lough Derg.
1133	Lusk plundered by men of Meath.
1139	St. Mary's Abbey, Dublin, officially founded as a Benedictine house.
1140–48	St. Mary's Abbey of the Augustinian Canons founded at Kells under St. Malachy.
1142	Mellifont founded by St. Malachy as Ireland's first Cistercian abbey.
1143-48	Drumlane Abbey, now St. Mary's Abbey, transferred to the Augustinians and made subject to St. Mary's Abbey, Kells, by St. Malachy.
1144–1195	Augustinian (Arrouaise) nuns in Lusk.
1146/7(c.)	Knight Owein reportedly visits St. Patrick's Purgatory. (See 1185 c.)
1147	St. Mary's Abbey, Dublin, transferred to the Cistercians by St. Malachy.
1148	St. Malachy dies, Nov. 2.
1152	Synod of Kells (at Mellifont). Kells Abbey becomes a cathedral.
1152	According to one account, Dervorgill, daughter of the king of Meath, writes to her lover Diarmaid MacMurrough that her husband has gone on pilgrimage to St. Patrick's Purgatory, so it's a good time to come fetch her. If authentic, this would be the earliest mention of St. Patrick's Purgatory.

1156	Slane Abbey plundered; Kells burned.
1157	Devenish burned.
1161	Slane Abbey plundered.
1170 (c.)	Anonymous knight reportedly visits St. Patrick's Purgatory. (*See* 1200.)
1170	Slane Abbey plundered; Kells and Castlekeeran burned.
1175	Transept begun at Christ Church or Priory of the Holy Trinity, Dublin.
1180	St. Laurence O'Toole dies.
1185 (c.)	H. of Saltrey's account of Knight Owein's visit in the *Tractatus de Purgatorio Sancti Patricii*. The earliest verified mention of St. Patrick's Purgatory.
1185	Jocelin of Furness thinks the Purgatory is on Croagh Patrick and mentions that pilgrims believe if they endure the night they will never enter hell.
1192	Stone church built at St. Patrick's site, Dublin, dedicated to God, the Blessed Virgin and St. Patrick.
1196	*Annals of the Four Masters* mentions St. Patrick's Purgatory.
1199	St. Malachy, first Irish saint canonized in Rome.
1200	Giraldus Cambrensis mentions St. Patrick's Purgatory in the *Topographia Hiberniae*.
1200 (c.)	Peter of Cornwall reports the c.1170 visit by the anonymous knight to St. Patrick's Purgatory. Church on White Island built
1206 (c.)	Abbey of St. Mary d'Urso, Drogheda, founded.
1213	St. Patrick's Dublin becomes a cathedral.
1224	Dominican friary of St. Mary Magdalene founded in Drogheda.
1237/9	Holy Trinity Abbey founded on Trinity Island.
1245	Maître Gossouin in *L'Image du Monde* describes the island of St. Patrick's Purgatory as a mountain of sulphur that burns day and night.
1246	Extensive damage to Drumlane Abbey.
1253 (c.)	Matthew Paris's account of Knight Owein's visit in the *Historia Anglorum*.
1254	New Gothic church at St. Patrick's Cathedral, Dublin.
1260 (c.)	Jacobus de Voraigne in the *Golden Legend* tells how the Lord showed the pit to St. Patrick. Describes the experiences in the Purgatory of a man identified only as Nicholas, and tells of pilgrims who entered the Purgatory and never came back, and of those who

	will have no more pain or punishment as a result of their pilgrimage.
1261	Stephen of Bourbon's account of Knight Owein's visit.
1283	Chapter house, dormitory and cloister of Christ Church Cathedral, Dublin, destroyed by fire.
1300	St. Mary d'Urso, Drogheda, by this time a house of the Crutched Friars.
1315	Kells burned.
1326	Steeple damaged at Christ Church Cathedral, Dublin.
1345	*Annals of the Four Masters* mentions St. Patrick's Purgatory.
1346 (c.)	Fresco of St. Patrick's Purgatory in the Convent of S. Francesco, Todi.
1350 (c.)	Ranulf Higden provides brief description of the Purgatory in his *Polychronicon*.
1352 (ante)	Sire de Beaujeu visits St. Patrick's Purgatory.
1353	George Grissaphan of Hungary visits St. Patrick's Purgatory.
1358	Louis d'Auxerre and Nicholas Beccari of Ferrara visit St. Patrick's Purgatory. A certain Malatesta de Rimini (l'Ungaro) visits St. Patrick's Purgatory reportedly in penance for having quarreled with the pope.
1359 (ante)	Taddeo Gualandi of Pisa visits St. Patrick's Purgatory.
1360	Devenish burned.
1365	Guido Cissi and John Bonham visit St. Patrick's Purgatory.
1394–95	Sir William Lisle and another English knight visit St. Patrick's Purgatory.
1395	*Annals of the Four Masters* mentions St. Patrick's Purgatory.
1397	Ramon de Perellós and William, lord of Corsy, visit St. Patrick's Purgatory.
1399	John of Brederode visits St. Patrick's Purgatory.
1400 (c.)	German monk of the order to St. Bernard visits St. Patrick's Purgatory. Old cathedral at Kilmore built.
1409	William of Stranton visits St. Patrick's Purgatory.
1411 (ante)	Antonio da Focha, a priest of Rome, visits St. Patrick's Purgatory.
1411	Antonio Mannini and Laurence Rathold visit St. Patrick's Purgatory.
1412 (ante)	Eugene O'Brien of England visits St. Patrick's Purgatory.
1421	Guillebert de Lannoy visits the Holy Land.

1430	Guillebert de Lannoy visits St. Patrick's Purgatory.
1431	Extensive damage to Drumlane Abbey.
1434	Kilmore becomes an episcopal seat.
1440	*Annals of the Four Masters* mentions St. Patrick's Purgatory.
1446	Conrad von Scharnachthal visits St. Patrick's Purgatory.
1447	Aghalurcher church remodeled.
1449	Church on Devenish rebuilt.
1450 (c.)	Canon of Waterford visits St. Patrick's Purgatory.
1460	John de Banste of Bruges visits St. Patrick's Purgatory.
1461	Steeple damaged at Christ Church Cathedral, Dublin.
1469	*Annals of the Four Masters* mentions St. Patrick's Purgatory.
1484	Aghalurcher church abandoned after a murder on the altar.
1485	Jean Garry and François Proty, priests of Lyons (and their boy Jean Burgey) visit St. Patrick's Purgatory.
1486	Dionysius the Carthusian recounts Owein's experience in the otherworld, which he enters from the cave (*Quatuor novissima*).
1489	John Bermyngham and William Bramery visit St. Patrick's Purgatory.
1494 (ante)	Blasius Biragus visits St. Patrick's Purgatory.
1494-97 (c.)	Monk of Eymstadt visits St. Patrick's Purgatory; a cave is closed.
1497	A cave at St. Patrick's Purgatory is closed, according to the *Annals of Ulster*.
1500 (c.)	Lusk Round Tower incorporated into belfry.
1504	*Annals of the Four Masters* mentions St. Patrick's Purgatory.
1506	Peter de Navalibus reported in his *Catalogus sanctorum* that Patrick drew a circle with his crozier and the earth opened up to reveal a deep pit, the place of Purgatory.
1507	12 August, document by Master Donatus Magrahe, prior of St. Patrick's Purgatory, on indulgences. Nylanus O'Leden visits St. Patrick's Purgatory.
1512	Franciscan friary at Slane.
1516	Anonmous knight of France visits St. Patrick's Purgatory .
1517	Francesco Chiericati visits St. Patrick's Purgatory; sees Guarino of Durazzo's name in a book there. Martin Luther begins Protestant Reformation.

1519   St. Mary d'Urso, Drogheda, a house of the
            Observantine Friars.
1536   Henry VIII begins the dissolution of the monasteries.
1538   Relics of Christ Church, Dublin, including the
            renowned Speaking Crucifix and the Staff of Jesus,
            publicly burned.
1539   Mellifont Abbey and St. Mary's Abbey, Kells,
            dissolved.
1540   St. Mary Magdalene Abbey, Drogheda, surrendered.
1549   James Melville records that in this year he was a page
            to Jean de Monluc, bishop of Valence, when he visited
            St. Patrick's Purgatory.
1551   Holy Trinity Abbey, Trinity Island, dissolved.
1556   St. Mary d'Urso Abbey, Drogheda, suppressed.
1562   Nave vaulting collapses at Christ Church Cathedral,
            Dublin.
1570   Edmund Campion reports on a priest who had visited
            St. Patrick's Purgatory.
1570/71   Drumlane Abbey dissolved.
1578   Raphael Holinshed gave a synopsis of some of the
            literary history of St. Patrick's Purgatory.
1587   Richard Stanhurst mentions in his *Life of St. Patrick*
            that St. Patrick's Purgatory was frequented by
            travelers from foreign countries.
1600   An anonymous pilgrim to St. Patrick's Purgatory
            mentions that there were many pilgrims, both lay
            and clerical.
1600 (c.)   Mícheál Ó Cléirigh, chief author of the *Annals of the
            of the Four Masters*, describes the Round of Penance
            for Station Island. Tadhg Buide Magrath and Giolla
            Riabhach O'Kelly visit St. Patrick's Purgatory.
1603   An inquisition on Saints Island for Nov. 26, says that
            St. Patrick's Purgatory is in much decay and for many
            years has been totally abandoned and dissolved.
            However, there is apparently confusion here between
            the islands, since the ruined island is described as 10
            acres, and that would indicate the larger island, Saints
            Island and not St. Patrick's Purgatory on Station Island.
1607   Devenish abandoned by this time.
1630   The *Martyrology of Donegal* reports that at the eastern
            extremity of the lake are St. Patrick's Purgatory and
            Dabheoc's Island. And there is also a monastery at
            the western extremity.

1631	March 11, Hugh O'Reilly, archbishop of Armagh writes a letter asking Rome to confirm the Franciscans at Lough Derg because of the "innumerable crowds of pilgrims," but scarcity of clergy to meet their needs.
1632	St. Patrick's Purgatory officially suppressed. William Stuart attempts unsuccessfully to close down St. Patrick's Purgatory. Then James Spottiswoode, bishop (of Clogher?) demolishes everything on Station Island in one day: Oct. 25.
1638	Henrietta Maria, queen consort of England, Scotland and Ireland writes to Lord Wenworth asking him to re-open the Purgatory. He writes back to say, since it was so recently closed, and by the privy council, it's best to let things cool down a bit.
1648	Giovanni Battista Rinnucinni, papal nuncio, unsuccessfully attempts to reestablish St. Patrick's Purgatory during the Irish Confederate Wars.
1652	*Annals of the Four Masters* mentions St. Patrick's Purgatory.
1666	Map of the Island of the Purgatorium of St. Patrick in *Lyra Hibernica* by Fr. Thomas Carve.
1682	Thomas Knox states that there used to be so many pilgrims that the ferry to the island brought in 200 pounds sterling/year.
1688	Kells Market Cross moved from monastery grounds to town crossroads.
1693	Ludovicus Pyrhus of Brittany attempts excavation of Saints/Station Island.
1702	Earliest surviving penal crucifix from St. Patrick's Purgatory.
1710	Franciscans arrived at Lough Derg.
1763	Franciscans build priory of St. Mary of the Angels on Station Island.
1780	St. Patrick's Church, also referred to as the Prison Chapel, built on Station Island.
1785	Diocese of Clogher begins appointing secular priests to administer Station Island.
1813	St. Mary of the Angels rebuilt on Station Island.
1860	New cathedral at Kilmore built with doorway from Holy Trinity incorporated into vestry door.
1870	St. Mary of the Angels rebuilt again on Station Island.
1877	St. Nennid's Bell sold at auction, disappears.

1880	Large hospice (now the Men's Dormitory) built on Station Island.
1891	Lough Erne shrines discovered.
1899	Ernest Becker in *A Contribution to the Study of Medieval Legends* says that the cave had a reputation for being an entrance to "Purgatory."
1901	Excavations on medieval remains at St. Patrick's Cathedral, Dublin.
1905	John Healey says that St. Patrick's Cave was not on Station Island in Lough Derg but on Saints Island, which was sometimes Island Dabheog.
1910–12	Women's hospice built on Station Island.
1929	A new St. Patrick's Church built on Station Island.
1931	J.F. Kenney, in *Sources for the Early History of Ireland,* reports on the continuing role of Patrick as psychopomp for Christians.
1930s	Bed of St. Columcille goes missing at about this time from Kells.
1959	Excavations at White Island show the church site previously occupied by a wooden structure.
1989	Excavations of St. Mary d'Urso, Drogheda.
1997	Kells Market Cross restored and moved to its present location outside the courthouse after a traffic accident damaged the base.
2000	Women's hospice demolished on Station Island.
2003	St. Mary of the Angels on Station Island restored to 1860 construction.
2005	Davog House built on Station Island on site of demolished women's hospice.

Mattock River at Mellifont Abbey.

BIBLIOGRAPHY

*Our comprehensive bibliography on the legend of St. Patrick's
Purgatory can be found on the web at
http://www.hell-on-line.org/BibPatrick.html, including:
Bibliographical Works, Sources and Studies.*

Aalen, F.H.A, Kevin Whelan, and Matthew Stout. *Atlas of the Irish Rural Landscape.* Cork: Cork University Press, 1997.

Adamnan, and Marjorie Ogilvie Anderson. *Adomnan's Life of Columba.* Oxford Medieval Texts. Oxford: Clarendon Press, 1990.

Badone, Ellen, and Sharon R. Roseman. *Intersecting Journeys: The Anthropology of Pilgrimage and Tourism.* Urbana: University of Illinois Press, 2004.

Battersby, William. *A Walk around Kells.* Navan, Co. Meath: William Battersby, 2000.

Bieler, Ludwig. *The Irish Penitentials.* Scriptores Latini Hiberniae, v. 5. Dublin: Dublin Institute for Advanced Studies, 1975.

Bitel, Lisa M. *Isle of the Saints: Monastic Settlement and Christian Community in Early Ireland.* Ithaca: Cornell University Press, 1990.

Bourke, Cormac. *Patrick: The Archaeology of a Saint.* Belfast: H.M.S.O., 1993.

—. "Medieval Metalwork from the Diocese of Clogher." In *History of the Diocese of Clogher,* ed. by Henry A. Jefferies. Dublin: Four Courts Press, 2005, 25-40.

Boylan, Henry. *A Valley of Kings, the Boyne: Five Thousand Years of History.* Dublin: O'Brien Press, 1988.

Bradley, John. *The Topography and Layout of Medieval Drogheda.* Aspects of the History of Drogheda 1. [Drogheda]: Old Drogheda Society, 1997.

Brown, Peter Robert Lamont. *The Cult of the Saints: Its Rise and Function in Latin Christianity.* Chicago: University of Chicago Press, 1981.

Carville, Geraldine. *The Occupation of Celtic Sites in Medieval Ireland by the Canons Regular of St. Augustine and the Cistercians.* Cistercian Studies 56. Kalamazoo, MI: Cistercian Publications, 1982.

Casey, Christine, and Alistair Rowan. *North Leinster.* The Buildings of Ireland. New Haven: Yale University Press, 2002.

Chambers, Richard. *White Island: History and Mystery.* Private printing, 2002.

Charles-Edwards, T.-M. *Early Christian Ireland*. Cambridge: Cambridge University Press, 2000.

Coleman, Simon, and John Eade. *Reframing Pilgrimage: Cultures in Motion*. London: Routledge, 2004.

Coleman, Simon, and John Elsner. *Pilgrimage: Past and Present in the World Religions*. Cambridge: Harvard University Press, 1995.

Colmcille, Father O.C.S.O. *The Story of Mellifont*. Dublin: M.H. Gill, 1958.

Craig, Leigh Ann. *Wandering Women and Holy Matrons: Women As Pilgrims in the Later Middle Ages*. Leiden: Brill, 2009.

Crawford, H.S. "A Descriptive List of Irish Shrines and Reliquaries." *Journal of the Royal Society of Antiquaries of Ireland* 52 (1923): 74–93, 151–76.

Crawford, John and Raymond Gillespie, eds. *St. Patrick's Cathedral, Dublin*. Dublin: Four Courts Press, 2009.

Cunningham, Bernadette, and Raymond Gillespie. "The Lough Derg Pilgrimage in the Age of the Counter-Reformation." *Éire-Ireland* 39.3–4 (2004): 167-79.

Cunningham, John B. *Lough Derg, Legendary Pilgrimage*. Monaghan, Ireland: R. & S. Printers, 1984.

—. *Monasteries and Early Church Sites of the River Erne*. N.p.: Cumann Cléir Chlochair, 2000.

Davidson, Linda Kay, and Maryjane Dunn. *Pilgrimage in the Middle Ages: A Research Guide*. Garland Medieval Bibliographies 16. New York: Garland, 1993.

Edwards, Nancy. *The Archaeology of Early Medieval Ireland*. Philadelphia: University of Pennsylvania Press, 1990.

Fentress, James, and Chris Wickham. *Social Memory: New Perspectives on the Past*. Oxford: Blackwell, 1992.

Finucane, Ronald C. *Miracles and Pilgrims: Popular Beliefs in Medieval England*. Basingstoke: Macmillan, 1995.

Flynn, Laurence J. *Lough Derg, County Donegal: St. Patrick's Purgatory*. [Dublin]: [Eason], 1987.

Gardiner, Eileen. *Visions of Heaven and Hell Before Dante*. New York: Italica Press, 1989.

—. *Medieval Visions of Heaven and Hell: A Sourcebook*. New York: Garland, 1993.

—. Hell-on-Line. http://www.hell-on-line.org/

—. The Pilgrim's Way to St. Patrick's Purgatory. http://www.pilgrimswaytopurgatory.org/

Geary, Patrick J. *Furta Sacra: Thefts of Relics in the Central Middle Ages*. Princeton: Princeton University Press, 1978.

—. *Phantoms of Remembrance: Memory and Oblivion at the End of the First Millennium*. Princeton, N.J.: Princeton University Press, 1994.

Gwynn, Aubrey, and R. Neville Hadcock. *Medieval Religious Houses: Ireland. With an Appendix to Early Sites*. Harlow: Longman, 1970.

Hadcock, R. Neville, and Ordnance Survey (Ireland). *Monastic Ireland*. Dublin: Ordnance Survey Office, 1979.

Hamerow, Helena. *Early Medieval Settlements: The Archaeology of Rural Communities in Northwest Europe 400–900*. Oxford: Oxford University Press, 2002.

Halpin, Eoin. "Excavations at St. Mary d'Urso, Drogheda, County Louth." *Journal of the County Louth Archaeological (& Historical) Society* 23 (1996): 452-510.

Hamlin, Ann Elizabeth. *Devenish, Co. Fermanagh*. Belfast: Historic Monuments and Buildings Branch, Dept. of the Environment for Northern Ireland, 1979.

Harbison, Peter. *Guide to National and Historic Monuments of Ireland: Including a Selection of Other Monuments not in State Care*. Dublin: Gill and Macmillan, 1992.

—. *Pilgrimage in Ireland: The Monuments and the People*. Syracuse, NY: Syracuse University Press, 1992.

—. *The High Crosses of Ireland: An Iconographical and Photographic Survey*. Bonn: R. Habelt. 1992.

—. *The High Crosses of Ireland: With the Figure Sculptures Explained*. Drogheda: Boyne Valley Honey Company, 1994.

—, and Joss Lynam. *Lough Derg: The Shore by Saints Island, Co. Donegal*. The Heritage Council of Ireland. Kilkenny: Heritage Council, 2004.

—, Homan Potterton, and Jeanne Sheehy. *Irish Art and Architecture from Prehistory to the Present*. London: Thames and Hudson, 1978.

Haren, Michael, and Yolande de Pontfarcy. *The Medieval Pilgrimage to St. Patrick's Purgatory: Lough Derg and the European Tradition*. Enniskillen: Clogher Historical Society, 1988.

Herbert, Máire. *Iona, Kells, and Derry: The History and Hagiography of the Monastic Familia of Columba*. Dublin: Four Courts Press, 1996.

Howard, Donald Roy. *Writers and Pilgrims: Medieval Pilgrimage Narratives and Their Posterity*. Berkeley: University of California Press, 1980.

Lalor, Brian. *The Irish Round Tower*. Cork: Collins, 2005.

Lannoy, Ghillebert de, Charles Potvin, and Jean-Charles Houzeau. *Œuvres de Ghillebert de Lannoy, voyageur, diplomate et moraliste*.

Siècle littéraire des ducs de Bourgogne. Louvain: P. et J. Lefever, 1878.

Lucas, A.T. "'Penal' Crucifixes." *Journal of the County Louth Archaeological Society* 8.2 (1954): 145–74.

— "The Social Role of Relics and Reliquaries in Ancient Ireland." *Journal of the Royal Society of Antiquaries of Ireland* 116 (1986): 5–37.

McClendon, Charles B. *The Origins of Medieval Architecture: Building in Europe, A.D 600-900.* New Haven: Yale University Press, 2005.

MacCotter, Paul. *Medieval Ireland: Territorial, Political, and Economic Divisions.* Dublin: Four Courts Press, 2008.

McGuinness, Joseph. *Saint Patrick's Purgatory, Lough Derg.* Dublin: Columba Press, 2000.

Macneill, John Thomas. *The Celtic Penitentials and Their Influence on Continental Christianity, a Dissertation.* Paris: É. Champion, 1923.

McNeill, John T., and Helena M. Gamer. *Medieval Handbooks of Penance: A Translation of the Principal "Libri Poenitentiales" and Selections from Related Documents.* Records of Western Civilization. New York: Columbia University Press, 1990.

Mac Tréinfhir, Noel. "The Todi Fresco and St. Patrick's Purgatory, Lough Derg." *Clogher Record* 12.2 (1986): 141–58.

Melczer, William. *The Pilgrim's Guide to Santiago de Compostela.* New York: Italica Press, 1993.

Mellifont Abbey Press. *Mellifont Abbey and Its Environs: An Illustrated Guide and History.* Louth: Mellifont Abbey Press, 1980.

Mellifont Abbey: Visitors' Guide. [Dublin]: Dept. of Arts, Heritage, Gaeltacht and the Islands, 1999.

Mould, Daphne Desiree Charlotte Pochin. *The Monasteries of Ireland: An Introduction.* London: B.T. Batsford, 1976.

Nichols, Francis Morgan, and Eileen Gardiner, eds. *Marvels of Rome.* New York: Italica Press, 1986.

O'Connor, Daniel. *St. Patrick's Purgatory, Lough Derg: Its History, Traditions, Legends, Antiquities, Topography and Scenic Surroundings. With Some Account of Its More Notable Pilgrims and a Detailed Description of the Authorised Devotions Performed at Its Venerable Shrine.* Dublin: J. Duffy, 1903.

Ó Cróinín, Dáibhí. *Early Medieval Ireland.* London and New York: Longman, 1995.

O'Donovan, Patrick F. *Archaeological Inventory of County Cavan.* Dublin: Stationery Office, 1995.

Ó Floinn, Raghnall. *Irish Shrines & Reliquaries of the Middle Ages.* Dublin: Country House, in association with the National Museum of Ireland, 1994.

—."The Bell of Saint Ninnid of Inishmacsaint, Lough Erne, Co. Fermanagh." In *The Modern Traveller to Our Past, Festschrift in Honour of Ann Hamlin.* Ed. by Marion Meek. N.p.: DPK, 2006, 145-49.

—. "The Soiscél Molaise." *Clogher Record* 13 (1989): 51–63.

O'Reilly, Patrick. "Drumlane Abbey" 1 & 2. *Breifny Antiquarian Society's Journal* 2.2 (1924), 2.3 (1925–26): 311-38.

Paor, Liam de, John Hunt, H.J. Plenderleith, and Michael Dolley. *Excavations at Mellifont Abbey, Co. Louth.* Dublin: Royal Irish Academy, 1969.

Parke, William K. *The Parish of Inishmacsaint.* Inishmacsaint, Co. Fermanagh: The Parish, 1982.

Picard, Jean-Michel. "The Italian Pilgrims.' In Haren, 1988, 169–90.

Pontfarcy, Yolande de. "The Historical Background to the Pilgrimage to Lough Derg." In Haren, 7–34.

Richter, Michael. *Medieval Ireland: The Enduring Tradition.* Dublin: Gill and Macmillan, 1988.

Roe, Helen M. *The High Crosses of Kells.* Meath: Meath Archaeological and Historical Society, 1966.

Rowan, Alistair. *North West Ulster.* The Buildings of Ireland. New Haven: Yale University Press, 2003.

Ryan, John. *Irish Monasticism: Origins and Early Development.* Dublin: Irish Academic Press, 1986.

Sharpe, R. *Medieval Irish Saints' Lives.* Oxford: Clarendon Press, 1991.

Spears, Arthur. *The Cult of Saint Catherine of Alexandria in Ireland.* Rathmullen: Rathmullen and District Local History Society, 2006.

Stalley, R.A. *Mellifont Abbey: A Study of Its Architectural History.* Proceedings of the Royal Irish Academy, Section C,80,14. Dublin: Royal Irish Academy, 1980.

Stokes, Whitley. *Lives of Saints, from the Book of Lismore.* Oxford: Clarendon Press, 1890.

Stout, Matthew. *The Irish Ringfort.* Irish Settlement Studies 5. Dublin: Four Courts Press, 1997.

Sumption, Jonathan. *Pilgrimage: An Image of Mediaeval Religion.* Totowa, New Jersey: Rowman and Littlefield, 1975.

Trench, C.E.F. *Slane.* Dublin: An Taisce, 1976.

Turner, Victor, and Edith Turner. *Image and Pilgrimage in Christian Culture.* New York: Columbia University Press, 1978.

Webb, Diana. *Medieval European Pilgrimage, c.700-c.1500.* Houndmills, Basingstoke, Hampshire: Palgrave, 2002.

Wood, Helen Lanigan, and Bill Porter. *Images of Stone.* [Enniskillen]: Fermanagh District Council in co-operation with the Arts Council of Northern Ireland, 1985.

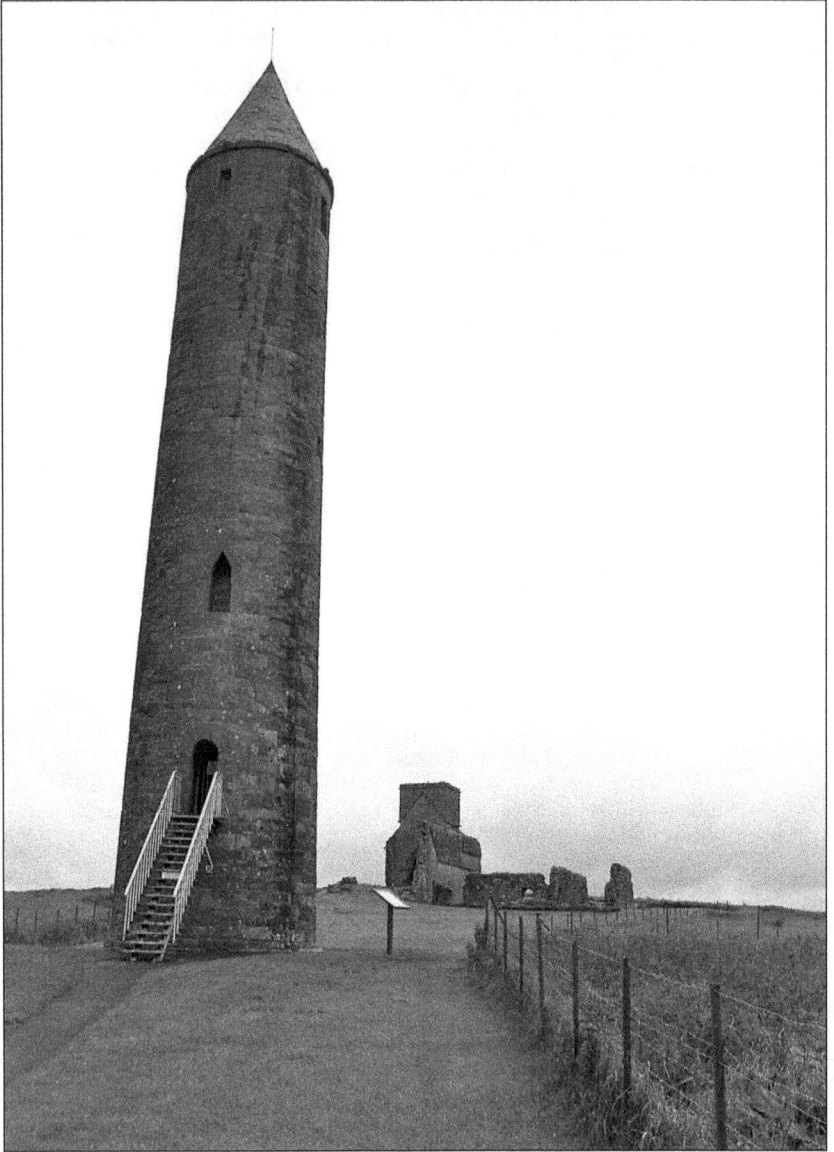

Devenish Round Tower.

INDEX

Italic page numbers indicate illustrations.

This Work Was Completed on June 25, 2010
at Italica Press, New York, New York.
It Was Set in Palatino and
Lithos and Printed on
55-lb. Natural Paper
in the U. S. A.
and E. U.

❖

West Cross, detail, Kells.

www.ingramcontent.com/pod-product-compliance
Lightning Source LLC
Chambersburg PA
CBHW022019090426
42739CB00006BA/203